SOCIAL CONSERVATIVES AND PARTY POLITICS IN CANADA AND THE UNITED STATES

The strength of the Tea Party and Religious Right in the United States, alongside the Harper Conservatives' stance on same-sex marriage and religious freedom in Canada, has many asking whether social conservatism has come to define the right wing of North American politics.

In this timely and penetrating book, James Farney provides the first full-length comparison of social conservatism in Canada and the United States from the sexual revolution to the present day. Based on archival research and extensive interviews, it traces the historic relationship between social conservatives and other right-wing groups. Farney illuminates why the American Republican Party was quicker to accept social conservatives as legitimate and valuable allies than the Conservative Party of Canada.

This book will be indispensable for understanding why a movement so powerful among American conservatives has been distinctively less important in Canada and how the character of Canadian conservatism means it will likely remain so.

JAMES FARNEY is an assistant professor in the Department of Political Science at the University of Regina.

Social Conservatives
and Party Politics in Canada
and the United States

JAMES FARNEY

UNIVERSITY OF TORONTO PRESS
Toronto Buffalo London

© University of Toronto Press 2012
Toronto   Buffalo   London
www.utppublishing.com
Printed in Canada

ISBN 978-1-4426-4431-1 (cloth)
ISBN 978-1-4426-1260-0 (paper)

Printed on acid-free, 100% post-consumer recycled paper with
vegetable-based inks.

Library and Archives Canada Cataloguing in Publication

Farney, James Harold
Social conservatives and party politics in Canada and the United States/James
Harold Farney.

Includes bibliographical references and index.
ISBN 978-1-4426-4431-1 (bound). – ISBN 978-1-4426-1260-0 (pbk.)

1. Conservatism – Canada – History.   2. Conservatism – United States –
History.   I. Title.

JC573.2.C3F37 2012   320.520971   C2012-901495-8

This book has been published with the help of a grant from the Canadian
Federation for the Humanities and Social Sciences, through the Aid to
Scholarly Publications Program, using funds provided by the Social Sciences
and Humanities Research Council of Canada.

University of Toronto Press acknowledges the financial assistance to its
publishing program of the Canada Council for the Arts and the Ontario Arts
Council.

 Canada Council   Conseil des Arts
for the Arts   du Canada    ONTARIO ARTS COUNCIL
                                CONSEIL DES ARTS DE L'ONTARIO

University of Toronto Press acknowledges the financial support of the
Government of Canada through the Canada Book Fund for its publishing
activities.

Contents

Preface

As I write this preface in the spring of 2012, contraception has become a significant issue in the Republican primary campaign, American courts at the state level are ruling on same-sex marriage as well as laws requiring ultrasounds before abortion, and state initiatives on same-sex marriage promise to be important in the fall general election. In Canada, a private member's bill seeking to define the start of human life, and court cases concerned with polygamous marriage, the legalization of prostitution, and freedom of religion, have brought renewed attention to the issues examined here. This book does not provide an up-to-the-minute treatment of these issues, but it does offer historical context and a theoretical blueprint for understanding them.

Such contextualization and theorizing are important, for social conservatism is often treated simply as a backlash – as the province of simple-minded religious believers who seek to roll the clock back to the 1950s. Such an image of social conservatives fails to explain why it has appealed to so many people or to shed light on the convoluted way in which our societies have sought to deal with the political implications of the sexual revolution and the important normative questions raised by social conservatism about the boundary between private choices, social mores, political decisions, and religious belief. Contention over these boundaries is unavoidable in liberal societies, but misunderstanding how they came about and their substantive nature can be avoided, and I hope this book helps resolve this.

Similarly, this volume tries to offer a better treatment of the distinctive nature of Canadian conservatism. By examining the most striking difference in the conservatisms of Canada and the United States – the relative strength of social conservatism in party politics –

this book seeks to explain the nature of the conservative coalition in both countries and the ways in which the different historical legacies of the two countries continue to shape the partisan options presented to their citizens. Particularly in Canada – where Stephen Harper's success at reshaping the federal political landscape has been remarkable – accurately understanding the nature of his party's ideology takes us a long way to understanding our political future.

This book began at the Political Science Department at the University of Toronto. Don Forbes was a wonderfully supportive mentor who let me run with an interesting story. Linda White, Rob Vipond, David Rayside, and David Laycock were very helpful readers; Victor Gomez, Joshua Hjartarson, Celine Mulhern, Reuven Scholzberg, Luc Turgeon, Jenn Wallner, and Steve White were constantly encouraging friends and colleagues. Most of the transformation of that draft into this book was done in 2009–10, when I was the Skelton-Clark Postdoctoral fellow at Queen's University. There, Robyn Brooks helped with the research for chapter 5; Oded Haklai, Scott Matthews, Royce Koop, and Elizabeth Goodyear-Grant were very encouraging colleagues; and Keith Banting was the very model of the supportive senior scholar. The final stages of the manuscript's preparation took place at the University of Regina, where I have found myself in a very supportive department. All three universities provided institutional support at one time or another. Daniel Quinlan, my editor at University of Toronto Press, has been tremendously encouraging and helpful.

My final debt of thanks is to my family. Christina has lived with this project almost as long as I have, but has shown considerably better humour and more patience with it. Bridget won't remember her signal contribution to it (accepting Hayek as a reasonable bedtime story) but has brought me tremendous joy during its writing.

SOCIAL CONSERVATIVES AND PARTY POLITICS IN CANADA AND THE UNITED STATES

Introduction

Social conservatives – that is, those conservatives whose political activities focus on topics like abortion and gay and lesbian rights – represent one conservative response to the sexual revolution of the 1960s. Like their progressive opponents, social conservatives accept that the 'personal is political' and advocate the use of state power to advance their beliefs about the proper ordering of society. Often, they also promote the application of religious mores to politics. This book's starting point is the observation that social conservatives have found different places in Canadian and American party politics. Understanding why this is the case means dealing with two puzzles: how the definition of conservatism has changed since the 1960s and how the different histories of Canadian and American conservatism framed the relationship between social conservatives and other conservatives as this shift took place. The first question – how the meaning of 'conservative' has changed since the 1960s – receives explicit attention in chapter 1. It identifies a group of conservatives, usually called social conservatives, who have emerged since the 1960s. They are distinguished from two older types of conservatives: traditionalist conservatives and laissez-faire conservatives. For different reasons, both traditionalists and laissez-faire conservatives are hesitant to treat issues like lesbian and gay rights or abortion as political or to allow explicit religious doctrine much political importance. Social conservatives, alternatively, argue that social changes in the sphere of personal morality create crucial political questions on which religious tradition often has much to say.

To say that social conservatives represent a new form of conservatism that has contributed a great deal to our image of the United States as a more conservative country than Canada is important.

Observing such a similarity naturally leads us to trace the different evolution of social conservatism, especially the relationship between social conservatives and other conservatives, in the two countries. This comparative-historical accounting of the evolution of social conservatism will not only help us understand the different paths of social conservatives, but should offer a more accurate characterization of Canadian conservatism as a whole than a number of recent accounts (MacDonald 2010, Warner 2010, Martin 2010), all of which, to one extent or another, have over-emphasized the power of social conservatism in Canada and, by so doing, overplayed the similarities between Canadian and American conservatism.[1]

With a typology of conservative subgroups developed, chapter 2 turns to examine American conservatism from the Second World War until the late 1970s. Unlike in Canada, and despite the American constitution's separation of church and state, conservatives in the United States generally accepted the social conservative concern with sexual morality and allowed that religious arguments had a place in the public square. Moreover, all sorts of conservatives shared the sense that they were outside the normal Republican party establishment. This made them eager to build alliances so as to enhance their chances of political success when they competed with liberal Republicans for control of the party.

Chapter 3 examines conservative mobilization in support of Ronald Reagan between 1978 and 1980 and the place of social conservatives in the Republican Party under Reagan and his successor, George H.W. Bush. It was during this time that social conservatives first made their presence felt in the Republican Party in a significant way. Reagan confirmed that there existed a legitimate place for social conservatives in the party while the Moral Majority and similar organizations proved to be powerful social movement actors. While social conservatives were not able to shift government policy as far as they had hoped during this period, the Reagan and Bush presidencies did see the cementing of the alliance between the conservative movement (with which social conservatives were full partners) and the Republican Party.

Chapter 4 looks at social conservatives in the Republican Party since 1993. The transition from social movement allies to co-partisans that occurred during this period, as social conservatives integrated themselves into the grass roots of the party, allowed social conservatives to consistently keep their concerns among the positions taken by the Republican Party but has also greatly limited their independence. It was during this organizational transformation that there was conflict over the place of social conservatives in the party. This conflict was but one part of a period of general debate among American conservatives about the meaning of conservatism. By the late 1990s these disputes seem to have been more or less resolved. Social conservatives moderated their policy demands and provided strong support for the party while other Republicans renewed their commitment to the recognition of social conservative concerns.

Until the late 1990s, the relationship between different types of Canadian conservatives was quite different from that in the United States. Chapter 5 examines the Progressive Conservative Party of Canada. It finds that the party defined social issues like abortion or gay and lesbian rights as moral issues that were improper subjects for political mobilization. This norm lasted from the emergence of social issues in 1968 until the collapse of the Progressive Conservatives in the 1993 election. Outside of party politics, the pro-life movement, the locus for social conservative activism at this time, was committed to a non-partisan approach and was internally divided, so it could offer little support to social conservatives in the party.

Chapter 6 examines the Reform Party. Here, the story is more complicated. Initially, the party's dominant approach to social issues (abortion still being the most prominent) was to declare them moral issues best decided by a referendum, not through partisan posturing. This populist preference for direct popular input affected social conservatives in a similar manner to the norm embodied in the Progressive Conservative Party. This changed during the mid-1990s, when gay rights replaced abortion as the dominant social issue and the party leadership's ability to enforce internal discipline declined. Reform then took a much more socially conservative position on gay rights than it had on abortion – a transition that marks the beginning of social conservative legitimacy on the Canadian right.

Reform's populism and its western roots prevented it from having a serious chance of forming the government. In an attempt to attract new supporters, Preston Manning, the Reform Party's founder and leader, initiated the United Alternative project in the late 1990s. While successful in creating a new party (the Canadian Alliance) this process also left Manning vulnerable to a leadership challenge. Stockwell Day, who defeated Manning in the resulting contest, gained a significant part of his support from social conservatives. Day's downfall, the rise of Stephen Harper, and the pressures facing the Canadian Alliance and the

Conservative Party of Canada are the topics of chapter 7. Despite the new parties' shared desire to form the government, and Day's rapid downfall, social conservatives enjoyed more prominence after the creation of the Canadian Alliance in 2000 than they ever had before. At least in part, this new prominence can be attributed to a change in the beliefs of Canadian conservatives generally, for many on the right came to recognize the concern of social conservatives as politically legitimate even if Canada's demographic realities and institutional configuration meant that social conservatives would never wield the political power that they do in the United States.

This focus on the legitimacy of social conservatism stands in a particular tradition of political science which emphasizes the influence that organizational forms have on political behaviour.[2] Other traditions of inquiry would emphasize other ways in which Canadian and American politics, such as political and religious cultures, legal traditions, federal structures, and social movement environments. The rest of the Introduction sets out both the specifics of the approach used here and the outlines of possible alternatives.

From the organizational perspective on political parties, American parties are similar to Canadian parties insofar as they are not mass parties, but they differ with respect to almost every other organizational feature (Young 2000). Indeed, from a comparative perspective, American parties sometimes scarcely seem to be organized parties at all (Katz and Kolodny 1994), as members of Congress and senators have a great deal of autonomy from the party's organization (Eldersveld and Walton 2000). Potential presidential candidates, in recent times, have generally drawn on networks of people personally loyal to them rather than on members of the party establishment for support (Wattenberg 1991). This situation gives outside social movements and policy entrepreneurs considerable opportunities to gain influence without the support of or sometimes even in opposition to the party's central organization. Not only do they have access, but – given weak party discipline – they can pursue a piecemeal strategy of winning influence over members of Congress or senators one at a time. Such influence can be gained either through conventional lobbying or through organizing in an electoral district to gain control of the party organization in that district (Wilcox 2006).

Canadian parties are – at least in contrast to their American counterparts – centralized organizations. They are tightly disciplined parties operating in a Westminster parliamentary system. This combination gives the party leader enormous power over decisions about personnel, policy, and strategy. This strength is compounded by the increasingly professionalized staff that supports the party leader but which is available to the rest of the party only in a much more limited way (Carty, Cross, and Young 2000). This disciplined parliamentary party is the only element of the party that can really be said to exist between elections, for the extra-parliamentary party is a short-lived campaigning device (Wolinetz 2002). The environmental pressures that cause convergence on this form of organization are great. Even the Reform Party, which initially sought to be less bureaucratic and less partisan, was eventually forced to conform to this model (Ellis 2005). The nature of Canadian party organization means that Canadian political parties are disciplined on questions of both office and policy, so that the views of the leader are critical to the position that the party takes (Carty 2002). The formal organization of Canadian parties, therefore, confronts groups like social conservatives with a clear challenge: the party's leadership has firm control of the agenda. Getting a social conservative position onto a party's agenda means convincing that party's leadership that it ought to be accepted. For, without that acceptance, only grass-roots mobilization strong enough to unseat a leader could hope to put new issues on the party's agenda.

This is not to say that Canadian parties are completely monolithic. As Perlin (1980) shows regarding the Progressive Conservatives and Ellis (2005) shows with respect to the Reform Party, such formal unity is often not fully realized. Factions do sometimes form, leaders are sometimes challenged (if often informally), and issues are placed on the agenda against the wishes of the leadership or in the face of what seems the electoral self-interest of the party. The question becomes which factions, with what type of challenge, on what type of issues, successfully challenge the leadership? Answering such questions means that it is necessary to do more than classify a party as franchise, cartel, cadre, or mass party (to mention only a few of the classic distinctions) on the basis of its formal organizational structure. Rather, it is necessary to work within a framework that allows a nuanced accounting of internal party dynamics – the sort of approach to political institutions generally described as the new institutionalism.[3] This approach views institutions as much more than collections of formal rules or organizational hierarchies. Instead, they represent particular ways of political organization that are defined in both formal and informal ways. They organize those active within them through

> collections of interrelated rules and routines that define appropriate be-
> havior in terms of relations between roles and situations. The process in-
> volves determining what the situation is, what role is being fulfilled, and
> what the obligations of that role in that situation are ... When they [mem-
> bers of an institution] encounter a new situation, they try to associate it
> with a situation for which rules already exist. (March and Olsen 1989, 160)

Action within an institution is about questions of correct identity, obli-
gations, shared assumptions, and duties defined both in formal organizational rules and, our focus here, informal norms of appropriateness.
This approach allows that parties are influenced by external factors
such as popular opinion, political events, and the nature of the competition they face, but treats them as more or less autonomous agents
whose interactions with their environment is neither entirely reactive
nor determined completely by that environment. Instead, parties are
understood as the institutional setting for debates and competition between different groups of partisans.

For our purposes, the central question in the reception of social conservatives concerns the appropriateness of their claims – were they
asking political questions in an appropriate way, as membership in
the Progressive Conservative or Republican parties (for example) implied? Social conservatives were rarely involved in full-scale debates
with other conservatives about what constituted the political parties
in which they were involved. Indeed, they seem to have taken the partisan organizations that structured their activity as given. What was
important, though, was what they and other conservatives thought
were appropriate topics for political parties to address. The norm about
the boundary between politics and morality held in conservative parties both constituted the conservative identity and defined certain be-
haviours as appropriate for those holding that identity. They helped
to define the actors who had interests to be pursued and identified the
constraints on how those actors could pursue their interests. Recognizing these features helps us to understand how conservative leaders
viewed public opinion and the nature of the competition they faced
with other parties; it does not discount such factors. Indeed, one would
hardly expect an institution to survive for long if the rules that defined
it were too out of touch with its environment or weakened it in relationship to its competitors. At the same time, given the path-dependent
logic inherent in this type of argument, norms may embody a view of
what is in the actors' best interest that is no longer entirely accurate.

When the gap between norms inherent in an institution and its environment becomes too great, institutional change can occur.[4]

Other approaches to the different place that social conservatives have found in Canadian and American politics would stress different factors, though none would offer us the insight into the nature of conservatism or internal party dynamics that the approach outlined above does. These other factors weave in and out of the account that follows, but it is worth stating the most important of them up front so as to make clear the other constraints within which conservative parties operated. These different contextual factors can be loosely grouped into differences in governmental institutions, different sociological contexts, and different systems of party competition.[5]

In addition to how differences between the presidential and parliamentary systems have influenced the structure of political parties, the broad institutional differences between Canada and the United States have created different opportunities for social conservatives to form alliances on the right. In both countries, litigation has become an important strategy for both sides in the debate over social issues. In Canada, this strategy became available only with the passage of the Charter of Rights and Freedoms in 1982. The Charter, which entrenched a bill of rights in the Canadian Constitution, is very popular in Canada. In the United States litigation is much more contentious, so that progressive court decisions have provided social conservatives common ground with other conservatives concerned with a governmental process that gives too much power to the courts. Futhermore, Canada's unitary judicial system and the nature of its constitutional division of powers have kept debates over gay and lesbian rights and abortion primarily at the federal level. This has prevented especially conservative provincial governments from making provincial laws more socially conservative or tweaking federal guidelines in a socially conservative manner. In the United States, alternatively, many of these issues are decided at the state level. This both creates more opportunities for social conservatives to influence policy and allows the movement to make progress in Alabama or North Dakota even when it loses ground in Massachusetts or New York State (Smith 1999).

Social movement scholars have made much of these broader institutional dissimilarities. For those who study political parties, a more customary area to focus on has been differences in the sociological makeup of the two countries. On the whole, Canadians are more socially liberal than Americans as well as being significantly less religious (Adams

2003). This obviously creates less fertile ground for social conservatives north of the border, a deficit that has been exaggerated by the different ways in which regionalism has interacted with the party system. In Canada, competition between the Liberals and Conservatives for office has been decided on the basis of one or the other party making gains in the suburbs around major metropolitan areas or in Quebec. In other words, the socially liberal areas of the country are the ones that conservatives need to appeal to if they want to win office. Since the 1960s in the United States, on the other hand, it has been either southern or border states (like Ohio) that have tipped the balance towards one party or another. These areas are much more socially conservative than the American average. Canadians are also much less religious. While defining terms is difficult here, 10–12 per cent of Canadians can be classified as evangelical Christians, compared with 25–33 per cent of Americans (Reimer 2003), and Canadian Roman Catholics have been less involved in socially conservative activities than their American counterparts (Byrnes 1991, Cuneo 1989). This means not only that there are more religious people in the United States who may find socially conservative positions appealing, but also that the religious networks that can mobilize believers are far denser in the United States than they are in Canada.

Finally, the party systems of Canada and the United States place social conservatives in subtly different situations in each country. In both Canada and the United States, competition for office is between a large party of the centre-left and one of the centre-right. This situation often leads both parties to appeal to the median voter, muting their ideological differences. In the United States, though, social issues were a key part of what drove conservatives (especially in the south) of the Democratic Party into the Republican camp. They were moving precisely because they were dissatisfied with the soft centre-left position the Democrats were taking and were unlikely to allow their new partisan hosts to take similar positions. In Canada, alternatively, social issues did not cause a rift with the Liberals to the same degree, and therefore appealing to the median voter from the right was a far less complicated concern. Where Canada's party system did allow an opening for social conservatives that was absent in the United States was in the Canadian system's greater openness to new parties. Canada's existing parties may be leader-dominated and difficult to influence, but they are vulnerable to challenges from new parties in ways that the Democrats and Republicans are not (Carty, Cross, and Young 2000). The Reform

Party, when it seized its opportunity in the late 1980s, took advantage of the openness of the Canadian party system to new parties with new ideas and, in the process, became the vehicle by which social conservatives entered the mainstream of Canadian conservatism. Such an effort was not needed in the United States but, had it been, it would have been far more difficult given the great stability of the American two-party system.

Recognizing the nature of the institutional and cultural contexts of Canadian and American social conservatism is important – no full treatment of the situation can safely ignore the influence of such factors. The historical evidence that follows, though, best fits with a theoretical account which emphasizes the interaction between the ideological beliefs of social conservatives and the implicit norms about the appropriate boundaries of politics embodied in conservative political parties. Particularly if the question of when social conservatism became a visible part of partisan appeals is considered important, we must give full attention to the ideational context within which other conservative actors responded to their claims. Underpinning this argument is the claim that social conservatism marked a change in conservative ideology about what the appropriate boundary of politics is seen to be. It is to the nature of this ideological innovation that we now turn.

1 Conservative Ideology and Social Change

The key to understanding how North American conservative parties responded to social change is to realize that conservatism is not a monolithic ideology. Instead, it should be understood as an ideological genus whose members share certain core values but to which numerous other possible commitments can be added. A leading scholar of ideology, Michael Freeden, has described the core of conservative ideology as (1) 'resistance to change, however unavoidable, unless it is perceived as organic and natural' and (2) 'an attempt to subordinate change to the belief that the laws and forces guiding human behavior have extra-human origins' (Freeden 1996, 344). This core means that conservatism is practically defined by its 'reaction to progressive ideology,' but that this reaction is 'substantively flexible' as conservatives react to challenges from different progressive ideologies (345).

Following this notion of conservatism as a mirror image or reactive ideology with a central concern with change, we can identify three types of change as major areas of concern for conservatives in twentieth-century North America: the breakdown of organic community in the face of rapid change, government intervention in the economy, and changes in gender roles and sexual mores. Emphasizing each of these concerns has produced a different type of conservative: traditionalist, laissez-faire, and social conservative. For the purposes of understanding the conservative reaction to social issues, two elements of each sort of conservatism are crucial: the appropriate boundary of the political and the appropriate sources of authority for political action. Only social conservatives wholeheartedly accept that politics includes matters of sexuality or the definition of the family ('the personal') and, either because of their view of human nature or their religious beliefs, have a clear and unambiguous vision of what sexual or family life ought to look like. For both laissez-faire and traditionalist conservatives, how to include religion in the public square and how to respond to social change are more ambiguous propositions. Before the 1960s, Canadian and American conservatism was predominantly laissez-faire with an element, stronger in Canada than the United States, of traditionalism. In Canada, the mixture of these elements took a form that denied social conservatives legitimacy in party politics until the early 1990s. In the United States, alternatively, the mixing of laissez-faire and traditionalist elements made American conservatism more amenable to social conservatives.

Traditionalists

Ideological strands recognizable as modern conservatism emerged in reaction to the French Revolution of 1789. What makes early conservatives different from reactionary defenders of *ancien regime* and of the divine right of kings is that conservatives were concerned with the orderly management of change while reactionaries simply sought a return to the pre-1789 situation. It was this concern that change be appropriately understood – rather than simply reversed or opposed – that makes Edmund Burke stand out as the founder of conservatism. Burke, especially in the English-speaking world, became something of a patron saint for conservatives, for his thought was far more amenable to the dominant liberalism of their societies. Indeed, Burke fits so easily with liberalism that Leo Strauss and George Grant – two influential twentieth-century conservatives – saw him as a part of the liberal problem rather than the conservative solution.

The debate over whether Burke was truly liberal or truly conservative cannot be resolved here. For our purposes, what is important is what traditionalist conservatives reading Burke have found in his pages. Those who have turned to Burke for guidance have found in his work themes of cooperation, community, hierarchy, authority, and tradition (Wiseman 2007, 21) or moderation, chivalry, prudence, and an untheoretical approach to politics (Forbes 2007, 61). These commitments differentiated conservatives from the nineteenth-century liberal opponents but were flexible enough for them to make common cause with liberals when socialism emerged as the major threat to tradition and community in the twentieth century. Aware of the inevitability of change (and of the desirability of some types of it) traditionalists sought to ensure that change was ordered, organic, and grounded in the wisdom of practice rather than in abstract ideology. Though an emphasis on tradition is the first thing that comes to mind when 'conservative' is mentioned, the set of principles that traditionalists articulated hardly amounts to a political program and has become vaguer as time progresses – a commitment to chivalry meant something definite in 1789 but in the 2000s addresses no central political issue. This vagueness is welcomed by some traditionalists, who see it as fitting with a literary tradition of lament, ruined churches, and desolate landscapes running from Samuel Coleridge to T.S. Eliot and J.R.R. Tolkien.

With the decline of inherited status as an organizing principle in society and the success of laissez-faire conservatism, traditionalist conservatism declined in importance. Its emphasis on measured change continues to be important, for it creates common ground on which conservatives can gather. This common ground had important implications for social conservatives, for traditionalism was largely silent about family and sexual life. This silence led to considerable ambiguity when social issues became politically important in the 1960s. To be sure, there was legislation governing divorce, homosexuality, reproduction, the age of consent, and other matters connected with sex and the family, but no significant movement or ideology made much of such things. They were not a topic of political debate and so, to the substantial degree that traditionalist conservatism articulates its beliefs only as it reacts to the claims of its opponents, conservatives spoke and thought little about them (Freeden 1996, 340–7).

There is no particular reason why the transition to political activism on social topics should have been difficult for traditionalists. As the treatment of the Canadian Progressive Conservative Party below shows, though, neither was it necessarily true that traditionalists would accept the political salience of social issues. In fact, many of them seem to have ranked maintaining a more circumscribed boundary to politics over using political means to defend traditional social mores. This sort of reaction might seem simply to be the product of strategic calculation or the contamination of conservative ideas with progressive ones. However, it is also the product of a feature of traditionalist thinking on these topics that, when applied to modern politics, makes it appear almost contradictory.

The challenge of relating traditionalist politics to changing social mores is clearly seen in the work of one of its leading contemporary exponents, Roger Scruton. His *The Meaning of Conservatism* (1984) attends to traditionalist 'dogma' (11) and makes clear that the natural enemies of traditionalist conservatives are liberals and their ideals of natural rights (15–16).[1] He defines conservatism as an amalgam of three key elements – authority, allegiance, and tradition – and seeks to defend an organic conception of the nation, as represented in two aspects: civil society and the state (27). Unlike many traditionalist conservatives, he tries to make explicit the relation between religion and politics and between the family and politics. His portrayal of these relationships – if taken to represent traditionalist thinking on these matters – shows why traditionalists could decide on no clear response to debate over social issues.

On religion, it is clear that Scruton is not overly concerned with the doctrines of whatever form of Christianity are established as the state or civil religion. This, he suggests, places him with conservative icons Burke and Disraeli (170), who were similarly unconcerned with the details of theology. What is important about religion is that it reminds one of the transcendent in a powerful way (170–1) and that it is established in order to 'reinforce the attachment of the citizen to the forms of civil life, and which turn his attention away from himself as individual, towards himself as social being . . . Be its fundamental doctrines true or false, it is nevertheless the most considerable of all political institutions whose identity is not identical with the authority of the state' (172). This vision of the role of the church is difficult to translate to North America – where religious diversity has long put such establishment outside the realm of consideration – but it also makes it difficult for a traditionalist to turn to some particular religious truth as a grounding for political action. The church is to be outside the state and is not to concern itself with politics. Its role is not so much to promote a specific religious doctrine as it is to serve as a prop to social stability generally.

Scruton's view of the family has some similar characteristics. He clearly desires to promote a conservative vision of the family (145). However, he does so because he believes that a model of family life centred on the care of children is the natural one and that families arise 'spontaneously, simply to do the peculiar and often indefinable things that they do, [so] it is impossible to lay down by fiat that they should incorporate as soon as formed. The law is forced nevertheless to recognize them' (146). If the role of the law is to recognize what emerges spontaneously, on what grounds would a traditionalist conservative argue against the recognition of different family structures, provided that the structures being recognized had been occurring for some time?

The answer, at least as provided by social conservatives, can come either by more directly applying religious belief to politics or by finding a single model of the 'natural' family that conservatives ought to promote. Neither of these moves, however, is implicit in the position taken by Scruton or by the sort of traditionalist conservative whose beliefs his work makes explicit. Indeed, such a political move would seem to run against their major claim – that religion and the family are autonomous institutions whose ends are distinct from those of political life (141–60).

Traditionalism plays an important part in the story that follows for, insofar as traditionalism was a formative and continuing influence on the Canadian Progressive Conservative Party, this indeterminacy on social and religious questions was an important source for the more limited Canadian vision of the bounds of politics. Traditionalist conservatism played a role in the United States, as well, but it was an imported ideology derived from a particular reading of Burke by figures like Russell Kirk after the Second World War. Primarily an intellectual enterprise, rather than a partisan persuasion, American traditionalism lacked the sense of noblesse oblige and affection for the welfare state that defined its Canadian and British equivalent. Far more abstract, American traditionalist conservatism meant:

> 1) Belief in a transcendent order, or body of natural law, which rules society as well as conscience. Political problems, at bottom, are religious and moral problems . . . 2) Affection for the proliferating variety and mystery of human existence . . . 3) Conviction that civilized society requires orders and classes, as against the notion of a 'classless society' . . . 4) Persuasion that freedom and property are closely linked . . . 5) Faith in prescription and distrust of 'sophisters, calculators, and economists' who would reconstruct society upon abstract designs. Custom, convention, and old prescription are checks both upon man's anarchic impulse and upon the innovator's lust for power . . . 6) Recognition that change may not be salutary reform. (Kirk 1953, 8–9)

This set of principles is far more specific than the beliefs that animated Canadian or British Tories. It is far more open to religion and, in its effort to be systematic, extends itself over all of society and conscience, as well as government, in ways that create an ideological openness to social conservatism. Traditionalists were not powerful in the Republican Party of the 1950s and 1960s, but they were an important element in the parallel conservative movement, into which they would help integrate social conservatives when the latter emerged during the 1970s.

Laissez-Faire Conservatives

By the 1960s, traditionalism was only an influence on, not the mainstream of, English-speaking conservatism. The mainstream was defined by what can be called laissez-faire conservatives. Laissez-faire conservatives are essentially classical liberals who fear that human freedom is threatened by the growth of government. In resisting this trend, these believers in the free market found themselves in the conservative camp as, from at least the 1930s onward, liberals and progressives saw the welfare state and central planning as key tools for human advancement. For laissez-faire conservatives, such central planning was only a way station on the road to totalitarianism. As a matter of practical politics, having similar opponents made an alliance between traditionalist conservatives and laissez-faire conservatives a relatively easy manner. At the level of principle, both groups shared a belief that the state should be limited and that many of the functions progressives wanted it to provide were more appropriate for civil society. Putting the same thing slightly differently, an alliance between conservatives and classical liberals was an easy one in societies like Canada and the United States, where the dominant political traditions were classically liberal ones – the principles of the free market and existing traditions were one and the same.

Belief in the desirability of small government and anti-communism made it easy for laissez-faire conservatives and traditionalists to act together but also obscured the very real differences between them. Laissez-faire conservatives are, at heart, liberals. They desire progress, rather than tradition's preservation, and emphasize freedom rather than order. As with traditionalists, the response to social change by laissez-faire conservatives was not clearly determined by their pre-existing beliefs – some parts of their thinking could make them look favourably on social conservatives while others were grounds for opposition to them. For some, their belief in individual choice and liberty suggested that the sexual revolution was a good thing – it would allow individuals free choice in their most intimate decisions. For others, even if they continued to be more concerned with economic policy and foreign affairs than with social issues, the sexual revolution represented another set of interventions into the organic ordering of society by elites in the courts, the media, and the educational system. Conservative action to resist or roll back these changes, in this second view, would not be unwarranted intervention but rather the removal of an outside influence on how people naturally order their private lives.

Given that laissez-faire conservatism is frequently lumped together with social conservatism, it is helpful to explore this indeterminancy at more depth by examining the approach's most careful political thinker, F.A. Hayek.[2] Before the Second World War, Hayek was a prominent member of the Austrian school of economics, a group of free traders who saw themselves as descendants of nineteenth-century liberals. They believed that a free-market approach could have prevented the economic problems that plagued Austria in the 1920s. Hayek moved from Vienna to the London School of Economics in 1931, where he became the most prominent critic of Keynes's technical economic work. Over the course of the 1930s, though, Hayek lost his argument with Keynes over the desirability of government intervention in the economy. For the thirty years after the Second World War, Keynes's vision of an economy managed by the government seemed the best way to moderate the downsides of the free market.

Over the rest of his long career – he was still publishing in the 1980s – Hayek worked more as a political theorist than as an economist. The most popular presentation of his thought, *The Road to Serfdom* (1944), is both a classic defence of the free market and an example of the powerful role that the fear of totalitarianism played in moving many free-market liberals towards conservatism. Central to Hayek's argument is a distinction between classical liberalism, with its guarantee of personal freedom (the primary goal of politics in his view), and collectivism, a genus of thought of which Nazism, Communism, and Keynesianism are only species. Hayek's argument rests on the assertion that, both historically and logically, political and social freedom is unattainable without economic freedom. For him, although the desire for significant government intervention in the economy often originates from praiseworthy motives, it is indefensible because of the threat to freedom it poses. The argument that totalitarianism was a threat to liberty motivated many postwar conservatives but does little to help us differentiate between different points on the political spectrum in liberal democracies. Where Hayek's arguments were more controversial, but also more useful in differentiating conservatives from liberals and social democrats, was his assertion that the welfare state – if its goal was conceived as promoting equality rather than alleviating need – would force the Western democracies towards totalitarianism. This warning was the practical message of *The Road to Serfdom*, but it was a problem Hayek explored more closely in *The Constitution of Liberty* (1960) and the three-volume *Law, Legislation, and Liberty* project (1973, 1976, and 1979).

The Constitution of Liberty was his effort to articulate and defend the liberal tradition, which sees that 'liberty is not merely one particular value but . . . the source and condition of most moral values' (6). This understanding is embodied in the traditions of most Western countries but is threatened by the expanding scope of the state that majoritarian democracy brings about, as 'liberalism . . . is concerned mainly with limiting the coercive powers of all government, whether democratic or not, whereas the dogmatic democrat knows only one limit to government – current majority opinion' (1960, 103). In a situation where many believe that the government represents the country and that it has a responsibility for ensuring economic equality, majority opinion can lead the government to discriminate between individuals as it pursues equality – the major threat to freedom. Hayek seeks to correct the two intellectual mistakes that lead to this position. The first is the belief that the government encompasses and should correct society. This, in his mind, is a fairly simple (though difficult to eradicate) mistake. Rather than embodying all of society, government must be understood as only one organization among many in society. As such, it must restrict itself to enforcing the rule of law and protecting the population from foreign aggression.

The more dangerous error is a fundamental misunderstanding of what the rule of law means that crept into the liberal tradition and which Hayek sought to correct in his *Law, Legislation, and Liberty* project. What the rule of law ought to protect, for Hayek, is the growth of spontaneous orders in society. The free market is the clearest example of such an order, but social mores can also be understood as such. It is within such spontaneous orders that freedom can exist (1960, 155). By changing the idea of law so that it is no longer simply rules that can be equally applied to all, but rather whatever the majority decides, liberal democracies have removed the key safeguard to freedom. Hayek's correction to this problem is to separate the making of law from the business of running government by making each task the responsibility of a different assembly (1979, 105).

While Hayek has been made a part of the conservative tradition, he saw himself as holding very different positions from either traditionalist conservatives or social conservatives. In a postscript to *The Constitution of Liberty* he explains at some length why he is not a conservative. To him, it is only a historical accident that those who seek to promote individual liberty are now considered conservatives. He understands conservatism as an 'attitude of opposition to drastic change' (1960, 397) but rejects it because it has no alternative to offer to the growing spread of totalitarianism. Classical liberalism offers a different future, conservatism just a different pace towards a future defined by collectivism. Unlike liberals, conservatives misunderstand the idea of a spontaneously ordered society by believing that it occurs only in the past and by attempting to squash it in the present by their emphasis on authority and tradition. Conservatives like authority more than is safe for freedom and too easily believe that state coercion would be safe if it was only used by them for their own ends. Fundamentally, 'conservatives deceive themselves when they blame the evils of our time on democracy. The chief evil is unlimited government' (1960, 407).

If he differentiates himself very clearly from traditionalists, Hayek is also clear that private morals are not matters for the state but are legitimate matters for social mores to speak to (1960, 146). This position is less protective of individual liberty from infringement by social pressure than some in the liberal tradition preferred – perhaps most notably J.S. Mill – but it is nonetheless a long way from social conservatism. In a brief discussion of the British Wolfenden Report (which recommended decriminalizing homosexuality), Hayek agreed with H.L.A Hart's defence of the report on the grounds that 'actions which affect nobody but the individuals who perform them ought not to be subject to the control of law, however strongly they may be regulated by custom and morals' (1976, 57). Since he sees social mores progressing through an evolutionary process, Hayek added that those societies whose mores 'regarding propagation' (1976, 57) were disadvantageous would simply be out-competed by other, more fertile societies. This position – that moral norms and social mores cannot be the substance of legislation – as clearly differentiates Hayek from social conservatives as his desire for progress through freedom differentiates him from traditionalists.

Beginning with Margaret Thatcher's victory in 1979 and followed by Ronald Reagan's 1980 election win, the rhetoric (if not always the reality) of laissez-faire conservatism defined the mainstream of a successful English-language conservative resurgence. The 1990s saw the continued strengthening of this economic consensus so that even 'third-way' leaders of the centre-left (like Jean Chrétien, Bill Clinton, and Tony

Blair) pursued the economic policies of their conservative predecessors. For our purposes, it is also worth noting that this type of conservative has been very successful at linking intellectuals to practical politics and policy. Through think tanks like the C.D. Howe Institute and the Fraser Institute in Canada or the American Enterprise Institute and Cato Institute in the United States, laissez-faire conservatives in both countries have successfully linked their economic theories to policy recommendations.

The desire to limit government power has made it easy for laissez-faire conservatives to make common cause with other sorts of conservatives on many issues. However, it has also meant that they have been hesitant to engage in conflicts over social issues. To many liberty-seeking conservatives, family and sexual matters are moral issues best left to the free choice of individuals. State action in such areas represents a grave infringement on liberty. In their view other problems – be they foreign policy or domestic economic policy – ought to be the focus of conservative activism. They are often quite concerned that the boundary between church and state is being ignored by social conservatives (Sullivan 2007). Others argue that the trend away from traditional mores is the result of state intervention and were that intervention removed a shift back to 'natural' patterns of family life would occur (Frum 1994, Novak 1982).

Laissez-faire conservatives – despite whatever alliances they can form with social conservatives – seek to ensure that government is not concerned with social matters. It should stay uninvolved in society, just as it ought to avoid involvement in the economy, because individuals making their own decisions will result in the optimal outcomes in both areas. For laissez-faire conservatives what is important is that government maintain its position of non-involvement and follow appropriate policy in areas that are genuinely political, such as foreign affairs. This means that the best social conservatives can hope for from their laissez-faire counterparts is an ambiguous concern with excessive state intervention in society. At worst, the underlying differences suggest the possibility of considerable conflict.

Social Conservatives

While traditionalists are concerned that change moves at the right speed and laissez-faire conservatives offer a vision of how to reconcile freedom with order, social conservatism is defined by a focus on the protection of traditional sexual morality and family structure. It emerged as a distinctive part of conservatism in the 1960s, when feminists and the gay liberation movement made the personal political. In its concern with tradition and social order, social conservatism can sometimes seem simply a variety of traditionalism, but it differs from traditionalism on two very important points. First, social conservatives believe that conservatives ought to use the state to defend their substantive positions on such matters as abortion, homosexuality, pornography, euthanasia, and what they refer to as 'radical feminism.' They do not forgo the defence of their substantive positions for the sake of keeping civil society and the state separate. Second, while there are secular social conservatives who envision the social role of religion in very similar terms to traditionalists, much of the movement is made up of religious believers who argue for the direct application of religious teaching to politics. Thus social conservatives give religion a different political role than the non-doctrinal establishment envisioned by traditionalists.

In making these political moves, social conservatives make at least one of two philosophical claims. The first, perhaps best put by Michael Novak, is that liberal democracy and capitalism must be underpinned by 'certain moral strengths, rooted in institutions like the family' (Novak 1982, 156). Prudential in form, this argument holds that the traditionally defined family and (more or less) traditionally circumscribed sexual life are necessary for healthy human communities and individuals. Treating family values as instruments for the pursuit of other goals has been an important point on which social conservatives and other types of conservatives can agree. This is important because it gives social conservatives a way to find common cause with other sorts of conservative as well as a means for social conservatives themselves to meld their social concerns with their generally conservative positions on other political issues. Novak, for example, has claimed to reconcile social conservatism and a laissez-faire commitment to the free market by showing how the virtues created in traditional families are necessary in a free society and in the free market. The second claim has been succinctly described by British literary critic Robert Grant:

Relations between persons are the stuff of morals; and morals, through the shared concept of 'justice,' seek dramatic confirmation and support in law (not to enforce them is to make the good look like fools). Moreover, law and culture reinforce each other: culture is underpinned by law, and law, at bottom, is simply culture in the guise . . . of necessity. Sexuality, then . . . is intimately bound up with matters that are ultimately political. (Grant 2000, 88)

This is a much stronger claim, for it posits that the state has a duty to promote traditional morality and means that social conservatives agree with progressives that family and sexual life are ultimately political. In the social conservative view what is wrong about the progressive stance is not the territory that it covers but the substance of the claims that progressives make. In bringing the state into such areas, social conservatives break with their laissez-faire conservative and traditionalist counterparts even as they defend traditional mores defining the family and sexual ethics.

In making either of these philosophic claims, social conservatives have had to take certain, contested, traditions of what the good society is and politicize them. Social conservatives argue that this politicization must occur because progressives have brought state power to bear so as to change social mores around sexuality and the family. Particularly irksome for social conservatives has been the use of the courts by progressives to promote their agenda when, as in most cases, democratically elected legislatures would not support progressive causes. Equally important, social conservatives have been willing to make political action on social issues a political priority. While allowing that the issues other conservatives are concerned about are also important, social conservatives see changes in family structures and social mores as particularly dangerous developments.

Though often portrayed as being solely a position held by religious believers, one can be secular and espouse socially conservative principles. A good example of a secular social conservative is the Canadian writer William Gairdner. Gairdner's first book, *The Trouble with Canada* (1990), articulated a frustration with the size of government and taxation that was shared by many populists and fiscal conservatives in the late 1980s and early 1990s.[3] It was his following book, *The War against the Family* (1992), that best represents both his own social conservatism and that of people who pursue a conservative vision of social virtue based on secular, rather than religious, principles.[4] Defending a vision of society based on freedom, family, and free enterprise, Gairdner argues for a political order that recognizes that politics is based on the individual but that the social order is founded on the family (Gairdner 1992, 585). In Canada, this social order was protected by English common law and traditional social mores. However, it has been threatened by an elite collectivism and totalitarianism rooted in the ideals of the French Revolution and embodied in the Charter of Rights and Freedoms. While Gairdner admits that much of the culture now deviates from the standards he espouses, he believes that what he argues for has historically been shown to be the only path to a healthy society.

Those who are social conservatives for religious reasons are usually conservative Roman Catholics, evangelical Protestants, or fundamentalist Protestants. While politically active American evangelicals (the religious right) have received the most attention, Catholics have also provided important personnel, financial, and intellectual resources to key social conservative causes. Despite a good deal of distrust between the different religious traditions, they share a belief that religious truth can be brought to bear on politics.[5] This belief, moreover, seems to be accepted by their more secular counterparts. Religious conservatives usually downplay the social justice teachings of Christianity and emphasize its implications for family and sexual life (cf. Novak 1982). The debates that have gone on around the political implications of Christian doctrine mean that many who articulate a conservative Christian position on, for example, sexual ethics, have difficulty describing themselves as conservatives because they see an expansive welfare state as the best way of meeting Christianity's traditional teachings of a duty towards the poor. Rather than equating all religious positions with conservatism, it is more accurate to think that those conservatives who are religiously inspired emphasize certain parts of their religion over others.

An excellent introduction to religious conservatism in North America is the 'Evangelicals and Catholics Together' statement signed by fifteen prominent theologians from both sides of the denominational divide.[6] The statement begins by emphasizing the unity of their faith in Christ, the importance of Scripture, and a shared affirmation of Christian doctrine as expressed in the Apostles Creed. It then expresses a hope that 'our unity in the love of Christ will become ever more evident as a sign to the world of God's reconciling power' (Colson and Neuhaus 1995, xx), despite a list of their significant theological differences. The bulk of the statement focuses on politics. Acknowledging that the basis of their thinking is Christ and his cause and a recent realization of the public responsibilities of their faith, the authors 'contend for the truth that politics, law and culture must be secured by moral truth' (xxiii). This must be contended because too many now 'deny that securing civil virtue is a benefit of religion' (xxiii). The statement celebrates religious freedom but expresses concern that that freedom is threatened by the manner in which the American constitution is now interpreted. An equally important problem in the law is legalized abortion, described as 'the leading edge of an encroaching culture of death' (xxv). The statement wants to see 'schools that transmit to coming generations our cultural heritage, which is inseparable from the formative influence of religion' (xxv), seeks to defend the free market, and argues for action to knock down barriers of religion, race, ethnicity, sex, and class. The statement concludes by setting some ground rules for evangelization in areas of the world where the two traditions compete with each other for converts.

One of the instigators of this document, Richard John Neuhaus, is probably the most prominent social conservative intellectual of a religious bent. His views on religiously motivated political action (taking abortion as the issue most in need of intervention) were expressed most fully in 1984's *The Naked Public Square*. Neuhaus argues that American political institutions were founded with religious motivations and cannot function without a religious underpinning. He also claims, as a normative matter, that politics is a cultural activity and that religion is at the heart of culture. Religious arguments and institutions have a place in political debate, and, equally important, the boundaries of what is political and what is not are quite blurred (1984, 27, 165). The problem, Neuhaus argues, is that religious organizations and viewpoints have been pushed out of political life by secular humanists who, while only a minority of the population, are the leading members of the culture- and opinion-shaping new class. Nowhere for him is the damage of this shift clearer than in the aftermath of *Roe v. Wade*. Not only is the situation in the United States regarding abortion immoral – for it allows for the large-scale killing of human beings – but it is also deeply undemocratic, for it is opposed by a majority of Americans (25–7). Such problems can only be resolved if religious arguments and actors are allowed back into the public square. This is not considered a threat to the separation of church and state because it entails not the removal of religious arguments or religious believers from the public square but the separation of religious institutions from political ones. For him, the separation of church and state is meant to ensure mutual institutional autonomy, not to remove religion from public discourse. For Neuhaus, and for many other social conservatives, such sanitizing is dangerous.

Whether they draw on religious or secular reasoning to support their position, social conservatives have been able to agree (generally) on a set of developments they oppose. Their most important concerns have been the decriminalization of abortion and the various ways in which legal and social acceptance has been extended to homosexuality. Pornography, euthanasia, and more radical forms of feminism have also been issues of serious ongoing concern for them. It is important to remember that social conservatives do not believe themselves to be pushing an agenda forward but as reacting to an undeserved and surprise attack on the virtues that they hold dear by those enraptured by the opportunity for the 'radical restructuring of society through centralized social engineering of the most insidious kind' (Gairdner 1990, 272).

Conclusion

While these tendencies are not mutually exclusive – indeed, most conservatives feel drawn to at least two of them – they do provide a basis for understanding the different arguments and intellectual traditions from which North American conservatives draw. Particularly important has been how, in response to the challenges posed by progressive thought, conservatives have rethought the relationships between state and market (the traditional public realm), sexual and domestic life (traditionally private), and civil society institutions. Traditionalists were caught in a difficult conceptual bind by social change. Many of them supported the traditional order of family life but saw it as defined naturally and by civil society institutions like churches. They agreed that these were areas of public concern but denied that they should be areas of political interest and were hesitant to turn to theology for solutions. More perceptive traditionalists realized that the liberalization of society would prevent this position from being maintained for long, but hoped for some shift in the cultural winds (e.g., Grant 1998, 4–12). More politically involved traditionalists – many Canadian Tories, for example – simply refused to acknowledge that a shift was occurring. Given that traditionalists had never fully expressed what the relationship between the state and the family ought to be, this refusal appeared as a norm that government leaders should not discuss social issues.

Laissez-faire conservatives have, by and large, followed a similar path. In keeping with traditional liberal reasoning, they have held that the government should refrain from interfering in the private lives of citizens. This was often matched with an argument that government action in any sphere of life ought to be restricted, so they can consistently argue that the government should have no role in the definition of marriage, for example (e.g., Sullivan 2007). Some laissez-faire conservatives have allowed that there should be a pushback against the special interests that use state power to promote a progressive agenda on social issues, but they desire to go no further than making the state a neutral arbitrator to such disputes – they definitely do not seek a state that promotes social virtue or religiosity.

Social conservatives, in contrast, have accepted that the sexual and domestic have become the grounds for government action and political mobilization. They have refused to accept older conservative norms that sought to keep these aspects of life out of politics. Instead, they try to enlist governments to protect their version of family life – a vision they often define in explicitly theological terms. Many would prefer that domestic life still fell under the jurisdiction of civil society institutions but, given the choice between preserving their preferred vision of the family and not using the power of government to promote their agenda, have chosen political action.

Social conservatism is characterized not only by the political defence of traditional ideas of family and sexual life, but also by a deep antipathy towards those who challenge these norms. Whether the program social conservatives articulate is rooted in religious belief or in a vision of what a healthy society looks like, they agree that the feminists and gay rights activists who challenge their views are undercutting the very foundation of society – the family. Against claims that family structures are time-bound social constructions, social conservatives have defended what they see as the natural definition of the family: a husband, wife, their children, and the right to life of those children.

2 American Conservatism before Ronald Reagan

Introduction

Since Ronald Reagan's 1980 presidential victory, social conservatism and the Religious Right have seemed to be permanent parts of American public life. However, the alliance of religion and conservatism is not a combination that is either natural or permanent in American politics. Rather, it is a post–Second World War phenomenon, the initial kernel of which was a coalition between right-wing Republicans and conservative intellectuals formed in the 1950s and 1960s. Unlike in Canada, the ideological composition, political organization, and electoral base of support that defined conservatism all provided room for social conservatives when they began to emerge in the early 1970s. Other conservatives might not always agree with the priority social conservatives gave to social issues, but they did see concerns about such issues as legitimate and were willing to allow religious beliefs a place in politics. Opposition to such commitments came from the 'liberal' group within the Republican Party – a group that was in severe decline by the late 1970s.

That social conservatives were recognized as legitimate from the time they emerged in the United States is an important reason for their political success there. It is not, however, the only reason. Social conservatism offered a way even for relatively centrist Republicans like Richard Nixon to appeal to white southern and Catholic voters (both traditionally Democrat voting blocs) in a way that had no parallel in Canada. Further, the porous nature of American parties offered significant room for the social movements that conservatives organized to gain influence within the Republican Party – efforts that the tightly disciplined

Progressive Conservative Party could easily reject. Clarifying the terms on which conservatives generally, and social conservatives in particular, built their alliance with the Republican Party in the 1950s, 60s, and 70s takes us a long way towards understanding the reasons for their success in the 1980s, 90s, and 2000s, for the ideological foundation of this alliance has remained remarkably unchanged since then.

Conservatives in the Republican Party

The oldest part of what became the conservative coalition was a group known as the Old Right or Taft Republicans, who formed the Congressional mainstay of the party during the 1930s, 40s, and 50s.[1] Generally from the midwest, they opposed New Deal economic policies, 'internationalist' foreign policy, and Communism. Successful congressionally (usually through an alliance with the conservative southern faction of the majority Democrats), the Old Right struggled with the liberal Republicans who controlled the party's presidential nomination and much of its national organization. By and large, Old Right Republicans were laissez-faire conservatives concerned about American expansion abroad. Their leader in the decade after the Second World War, Senator Robert A. Taft of Ohio, typified them in his

> ferocious loyalty to his party and distrust of the eastern financial establishment, which he suspected of collaboration with the New Deal and encouragement of intervention overseas. Taft further feared that the New Deal's centralization of government and intervention in economic affairs would stifle America's exceptional 'individualism.' (Reinhard 1983, 29)

During the 1940s and 1950s, when the Republicans were the minority party in Congress and the south was a Democratic preserve, the conservatives of the rural midwest and northeast provided much of the Republican Party's representation in Washington. As far as was politically feasible, they continued to oppose the expansion of government that had occurred during President Roosevelt's New Deal of the 1930s and tended towards isolationism in foreign policy. Universally anti-Communist, many had seen the primary Communist threat as a domestic one at the start of the Cold War and had supported Senator Joe McCarthy and his Committee on Un-American Activities. The world-wide spread of Communism, combined with the failure of McCarthy to find much evidence of domestic Communist subversion, made isolationism less and less popular among right-wing Republicans (as well as among the population at large) during the 1950s. Instead, right-wing Republicans began to call for an aggressively interventionist foreign policy to combat Communism abroad. In the decades to come, that United States foreign policy needed to take a very strong line against the Soviet Union would be a point of agreement for almost all conservatives (Ehrman 1995).

While successful in Congress, the conservative wing of the party was consistently defeated by the liberal, or establishment, wing in contests for the presidential nomination. These establishment Republicans preferred internationalist candidates who were also friendly towards the New Deal. Their support helped Wendell Wilkie (in 1940) and Thomas Dewey (in 1944 and 1948) win the Republican nomination. Eisenhower's 1952 and 1956 presidential victories pointed to a successful formula: a Republican presidential candidate should not threaten what the New Deal had established domestically, maintain the trust of big business, and stay committed to an internationalist foreign policy. Eisenhower's success also cemented the hold of the liberal wing on the national party, for his time in office was book-ended by his defeat of Robert Taft in 1952 and Nelson Rockefeller's (the quintessential liberal Republican) role as kingmaker in Richard Nixon's 1960 nomination victory (Reinhard 1983).

Conservative Republicans saw an opportunity in 1960 when Eisenhower stepped down. Eisenhower's vice-president, Richard Nixon, ultimately won the nomination, but conservatives with links to both the movement and the party tried to draft Arizona Senator Barry Goldwater. Goldwater refused, having already pledged his support to Nixon, but this attempted draft represents the first important sign of modern conservative organization within the Republican Party. Deeply involved in the group that tried to draft Goldwater in 1960 were individuals – like Clifton White and Brent Bozell – with close ties to the conservative intellectual movement. The same group of activists began organizing in 1962 for the 1964 nomination contest. White's fellow organizers invested a great deal of effort in quietly ensuring that conservatives would be selected as delegates to the Republican nominating convention. They were successful in the many states where delegates were selected by caucus and also raised considerable sums of money. This group hoped Goldwater would run, but they believed that even if he did not, their organizational effort would bring conservative activists from all over the country together, laying the groundwork for future victories. Throughout 1962 and 1963, though, Goldwater kept this group at arm's length.[2]

Goldwater agreed to run for the nomination in January 1964, even though, after President Kennedy's assassination, polls showed the Republican Party doing poorly. He won the Republican nomination after a hard-fought campaign against liberal Republican stalwart Nelson Rockefeller. Rockefeller's divorce and remarriage to a much younger woman during the campaign, as well as the effort that White and other conservative activists had put into organizing the grass roots of the party, proved decisive advantages for Goldwater. After his victory he did not reach out to liberals in the party. Instead, his acceptance speech called for ideological purity, claiming that 'extremism in the defense of liberty is no vice. And let me remind you also that moderation in the pursuit of justice is no virtue' (quoted in Reinhard 1983, 196). Goldwater followed upon this rhetoric by ensuring that key positions in the party's hierarchy went to conservatives and by choosing a fellow conservative, William Miller, as a running mate. As a result, Goldwater fought the election without the support of a powerful part of his party and with significant vulnerability to Lyndon Johnson's charge of extremism. He lost it in one of the biggest landslides in American history. After his defeat, liberals in the party took the opportunity to purge his appointees from the party organization (Reinhard 1983).

Strident, at times disorganized, and ultimately unsuccessful, Goldwater's 1964 campaign nevertheless marks the political emergence of modern American conservatism. Goldwater's principles are an excellent example of mainstream Republican conservatism in the mid-1960s. Goldwater stressed laissez-faire themes, but his way of doing so left room for religious appeals and concerns with social virtue.[3] The introduction to his campaign book, *The Conscience of a Conservative*, sets out his position:

> The root difference between the conservatives and the Liberals of today is that Conservatives take account of the *whole* man, while the Liberals tend to look only at the material side of man's nature. The Conservative believes that man is, in part, an economic, an animal creature; but that he is also a spiritual creature with spiritual needs and spiritual desires. What is more, these needs and desires reflect the *superior* side of man's nature, and thus take precedence over his economic wants. Conservatism therefore looks upon the enhancement of man's spiritual nature as the primary concern of political philosophy. (1965, 10–11; italics in original)

For Goldwater, taking account of men as whole creatures means that *'only a philosophy that takes into account the essential differences between men, and, accordingly, makes provision for developing the different potentialities of each man can claim to be in accord with Nature'* (11; italics in original). In the conservative view, man 'cannot be economically free . . . if he is enslaved politically' and 'every man, for his individual good and that of his society, is responsible for his own development' (12). These three founding principles mean that the conservative 'looks upon politics as the art of achieving the maximum amount of freedom for individuals that is consistent with the maintenance of the social order' (13).

Goldwater departed from traditionalist conservatives in the conservative movement in his judgment about the relative balance been order and freedom:

> In our day, order is pretty well taken care of. The delicate balance that ideally exists between freedom and order has long since tipped against freedom practically everywhere on earth . . . Thus, for the American Conservative, there is no difficulty in identifying the day's overriding political challenge: it is *to preserve and extend freedom.* As he surveys the various attitudes and institutions and laws that currently prevail in America, many questions will occur to him, but the Conservative's first concern will always be: *Are we maximizing freedom?* (14; italics in original)

These principles meant a defence of states' rights (27), spending cuts and lower taxes (65), an attack on 'welfarism' (85), and configuring education to pass on a tradition rather than to promote progress (86). Abroad, Goldwater called for a strategic offensive against the Communist bloc based on clear military superiority (125) and caution in dealings with the United Nations (114). In speeches during the primaries he called for a voluntary social security scheme and for a nuclear weapons policy that (under some circumstances) would release control over those weapons to theatre-level commanders.

Though he was defeated by Johnson in a landslide, Goldwater's campaign did have two bright spots for conservatives. By bringing together activists in the conservative movement with right-wing Republicans, it helped to cement the organizational formula that led to later conservative victories. Goldwater's campaign also marked the first significant Republican success in the Deep South since the Civil War. The party had tried during the 1950s to break into the south, but without much success. Goldwater's success was the result of a combination of the discontent of many white southerners with the civil rights programs of the Democratic Party and his firm espousal of states' rights in response. For many Republicans, this success pointed to the possibility of breaking the close alliance between southern voters and the Democratic Party. Republicans soon became adept at using socially conservative appeals to convince white southerners that it was now the Democrats that threatened the southern way of life.[4] Both Richard Nixon and Ronald Reagan would base much of their success on southern states – states that were solidly Republican in presidential voting by the 1980s and at the Congressional level by the 1990s.

While this appeal to white southerners benefited Goldwater's campaign and would pay big dividends late in the next decade, it also put the Republicans in a very difficult position on questions of race and civil rights. Theirs had traditionally been the anti-segregation party. This status had been taken away from them by the civil rights initiatives of Kennedy and Johnson and, because of a growing preference for laissez-faire federal policy and the attraction of the votes of white southerners, they made no serious effort to regain it. To the civil rights movement of the early 1960s, conservative Republicans responded with an espousal of states' rights. When a series of race riots swept major American cities in 1965 and 1967, the Republican response was that the nation needed more of an emphasis on law and order. Many working-class whites in the north (traditionally Democrats) found this stance very appealing (Flamm 2005).

Goldwater's campaign laid important long-run foundations for American conservatives, but his defeat was a setback for conservative Republicans in the short and mid-term. California Governor Ronald Reagan did run for the Republican nomination in 1968 as an out and out conservative, but most conservative Republicans (including Goldwater) supported Richard Nixon as the most conservative candidate likely to win. Conservatives did not like Nixon as much as they did Goldwater or Reagan, but they did prefer him to a centrist like George Romney or, worst of all, a liberal like Nelson Rockefeller. Conservatives were also somewhat satisfied by the willingness of Nixon's first vice-president, Spiro Agnew, to articulate conservative positions on some of the emerging social issues and by the presidential candidate's hawkish foreign policy positions.[5]

Nixon himself is best understood as a party loyalist who was willing to situate himself wherever seemed best for the Republican Party and his own career. He had entered the party in the late 1940s, supported the Civil Rights Act of 1957, and, during the 1950s, argued that the party ought to pursue African-American votes by being progressive on civil rights questions. As president, he supported the Equal Rights Amendment, instituted wage and price controls in 1971, and oversaw a considerable growth in social services. On foreign policy, Nixon was a consistent anti-Communist who was nevertheless willing to pursue a policy of détente with the Communist Chinese and the Soviet Union (Mason 2004).

This pragmatism resulted in occasional tensions between Nixon and conservatives both inside and outside the party. Even when relations were good, he was certainly not a favourite of the right in the way that Goldwater and Reagan were. That said, he did pursue a number of initiatives that conservatives favoured and worked hard to build good relations with them. He also won significant credit by campaigning vigorously for Goldwater in 1964 and pursued a 'Southern Strategy' in 1968 and 1972 that sought to follow up the opening that Goldwater's candidacy and civil rights had created for the Republicans in the south. This strategy sought to appeal to southerners without falling into the trap of an outright appeal for renewed segregation (Morgan 2002, Reichley 1981). An important part of it was to articulate a conservative position on social issues that also appealed to some working-class Catholics in the north – another traditional Democrat base that seemed amenable to Republican appeals. By 1972, Nixon added opposition to abortion rights and support for parochial schools to his repertoire in a further, successful, effort to appeal to Catholic voters (Critchlow 2007, 136).

Agnew's resignation over tax evasion and the far bigger scandal over the Watergate break-ins ended Nixon's presidency. Initially, the elevation of vice-president Gerald Ford to the presidency – and his selection of Nelson Rockefeller to be his vice-president – made it seem that conservatives would be shut out of the new administration. Looking more deeply into his appointments and policies, however, Reichley (1981) concluded that Ford was in a similar position to Nixon, a party stalwart whose ideology consisted of 'belief in the free enterprise system; support for strong national defense; wide latitude for local and state governments to make their own decisions; and minimum government interference in business-labour relations and the conduct of individual lives' (287).

Despite this openness to them, Ford's administration was criticized by conservatives. They were unhappy that he continued Nixon's foreign policy of détente and kept Henry Kissinger on as secretary of state. Kissinger and, by extension, Ford were criticized by conservatives for being insufficiently anti-Communist just as they worried that he did not do enough to limit the growth of goverment. Ford also faced intense pressure to move to the right on social issues. His ability to do so was complicated by his wife Betty's very public activism in pursuit of the Equal Rights Amendment (ERA) and her openly pro-choice position on abortion. Ford had supported the ERA while in Congress and, initially, gave White House support to the campaign for ratification of the amendment in the states. On abortion he initially equivocated but eventually instructed his solicitor general to support the Hyde amendment restricting federal funding on abortion before the Supreme Court.

While conservatives were gaining ground in the party, the aftermath of Watergate called into question the Republican Party's very viability. In 1974 and 1975 the party was at record lows in public opinion and had weak showings in the mid-term elections for Congress and the Senate. By 1975, some conservatives believed that forming a third, explicitly conservative, national party would be the best solution to this crisis (Reinhard 1983, 225). This project fizzled because the activists most interested in it (a group around Richard Viguerie) were unable to find any nationally prominent politician to front their efforts. They had hoped that Ronald Reagan would lead their new party, but he made it clear that he preferred to remain a Republican, even if it meant staying in a party headed by Gerald Ford.

Reagan had first come to prominence after his rousing 1964 speech in support of Goldwater.[6] Winning the governorship of California in 1966, he became the leading conservative presidential hopeful. He had run for the Republican nomination in 1968 but was defeated by Nixon. His 1976 campaign was stronger and helped by his solid record as governor. He lost the nomination only narrowly to Ford in 1976. It was the last time that a conservative would run with support based solely on the intellectual conservative movement and the Old Right of the Republican Party.[7] By the time of his successful 1980 campaign, Reagan was supported by new groups – the New Right and the Religious Right – that were able to mobilize significant numbers of voters by highlighting their concerns with the changes in American society. While Goldwater and Nixon had both benefited from the mobilization of these groups, it was in 1980 that these new groups really became close allies of the Republican Party. Reagan's great talent – the ability to present conservatism as the blueprint for a better future for America – became apparent in the 1980 election. In that contest, he both mobilized the new conservative coalition and reached out to non-committed voters in an unprecedented way.

The Conservative Movement

The success and nature of conservatism in the Republican Party were an important factor that created opportunities for social conservatives in American politics. The other organizational factor, whose importance was amplified by the strength that social movements and interests groups have in the American political system, was the emergence of a strong conservative movement that was open to social conservatism after the Second World War. Although they had some precursors in groups like the Southern Agrarians (Murphy 2001) and individuals like Albert J. Nock (1943), the network of conservative thinkers that grew up around William F. Buckley Jr and the *National Review* gained unprecedented influence in the Republican Party. This network promoted a self-conscious fusion of laissez-faire conservatism and traditionalism in ways open to religious arguments and to a concern with social virtue. The conservative intellectuals of the 1950s provided both the organizational and ideational kernel of what was to become an extensive set of conservative social movement organizations. As it grew to include an extensive network of grass-roots organizations, this movement would also become a vital source of activists and of financial support for the Republican Party.

While conservative journals of opinion had existed before, the popularity of the *National Review* (founded in 1955) and the prominence of its editor, William F. Buckley Jr, made its pages the practical exemplar of American conservatism for many years. Buckley was quite willing to use this power to rid the movement of what he saw as dangerous or mistaken elements, most notably members of the John Birch Society. He, and the group around him, sought to promote a reasonable and moderate ideology upon which both traditionalists and libertarians could agree. The fruits of these efforts were best expressed in a collection of essays published in 1964, *What Is Conservatism?* (Meyer 1964). This collection displayed the diversity of conservative thinking at the time, spoke to why conservatives of different varieties could expect to work together, and identified the specific policy concerns of movement conservatives. Meyer, the editor, identifies two types of conservatives, both of whom draw on the Western tradition and both of whom are deeply opposed to 'liberalism.' His division is one

> between those who abstract from the corpus of Western belief its stress upon freedom and upon the innate importance of the individual person (what we may call the 'libertarian' position) and those who . . . stress value and virtue and order (what we may call the 'traditionalist' position). (1964a, 8)

Meyer and other fusionists argued that these were not fundamentally different starting points but merely differences in emphasis. Since both sorts of conservatives needed the other if they were to fully represent the Western tradition, they could live in a creative tension.

In his contribution to the volume, William F. Buckley Jr identified the fundamental openness of the fusionists to religious reasoning. In a discussion of the resignation of one of *National Review*'s editors, an atheist who felt it against his principles to remain involved with the journal, Buckley states:

> Can you be a conservative and believe in God? Obviously. Can you be a conservative and not believe in God? This is an empirical essay, and so the answer is as obviously, yes. Can you be a conservative and despise God, and feel contempt for those who believe in him? I would say no . . . If one dismisses religion as intellectually contemptible, it becomes difficult to identify oneself wholly with a movement in which religion plays a vital role. (Buckley 1964, 222–3)

That said, religion was not the focus of *National Review* even though its editors and contributors were open to religious influences and believed that this attitude distinguished them from their liberal opponents. The journal's major concern was foreign policy, economics, and education. While disagreements did sometimes break out over questions like the Vietnam War, both wings of the conservative movement were strongly anti-Communist and agreed that an outward-looking American foreign policy was necessary if Communism was to be stopped. In economics, they were opposed to government intervention in the economy. There were disagreements between libertarians and traditionalists as to whether or not unfettered capitalism was entirely a good idea in theory, but, as a matter of practical politics, both groups agreed that the free market was the best solution to economic problems. The traditionalist part of the movement was most apparent in the position conservatives took on educational standards and prayer in schools (Nash 1976).

During the 1950s, these intellectuals had few ties to party politics. This changed in 1960, when a group associated with William Rusher, the publisher of the *National Review*, formed a committee to draft Barry Goldwater for the Republican presidential nomination. Although it was unsuccessful, the links formed by this committee allowed a close alliance between Goldwater and movement conservatives in 1964, when Goldwater did run. Buckley's brother-in-law, Brent Bozell II, ghost-wrote Goldwater's campaign book, and some of the other movement conservatives served as speech writers during the campaign. Also associated with the Goldwater campaign was an organization formed by some of the younger movement conservatives in 1960, the Young Americans for Freedom (YAF). This campus organization distributed conservative publications to students and was a significant forum in which young conservatives organized and networked. While often torn by ideological discord between libertarians and traditionalists, the YAF would provide significant numbers of foot soldiers for conservative campaigns during the next twenty years. An outgrowth of the YAF, the American Conservative Union, was founded after Goldwater's 1964 defeat to provide a similar forum for conservatives too old to remain active in what was essentially a student organization.

The conservative movement grew during the 1960s, but new issues emerged that both threatened to divide the movement and offered it new opportunities. Particularly divisive were debates over the Vietnam War, with some student conservatives of libertarian leanings joining left-wing anti-war groups and significant figures like Russell Kirk, Milton Friedman, and Barry Goldwater publicly opposing the draft while supporting the war. However, most conservatives opposed questioning of the war effort and called for all-out offensives against North Vietnam (Ehrman 1995, Nash 1976).

The campus unrest of the late 1960s and early 1970s, often initiated by student opposition to the Vietnam War, soon carried over into demands that curricula be changed and students given more voice in the running of universities. Campus unrest and the growing youth 'counterculture' reinforced traditionalist concerns that American education was failing. This campus unrest, as well as a preoccupation with American foreign policy, moved the group that became known as the neoconservatives to the right.[8] While not all neoconservatives were Republicans (Daniel Patrick Moynihan, who became Democratic senator for New York, is perhaps the best example of one who stayed in the Democratic Party), the 1960s and 1970s saw this group slowly become more and more a part of the conservative movement. Usually with backgrounds in the politics of the intellectual left, the neoconservatives preferred social scientific techniques to the philosophical or historical argumentation favoured by other conservative intellectuals. Their position on race, for example, was very much driven by the Moynihan Report's argument that the welfare state hurt African Americans more than it helped them by inflicting further damage on family structures. Neoconservatives claimed to take a similarly steely-eyed look at American foreign policy and argued that the country misunderstood its power in comparison to the Soviet Union and could, and should, take a harder line in the Cold War (Ehrman 1995).

During the late 1960s, race was the other major issue facing the United States.[9] The common position in the conservative movement was to defend the states' rights position but to deny that the freedom of the states to make their own decisions should be used to enforce segregation. Conservatives argued against federal action to protect the civil rights of African Americans in southern states not because they were opposed to the extension of civil rights (which they were not) but because such federal action was in violation of the division of powers set out in the constitution. This brought the conservative wing of the Republican Party closer to the policies on race favoured by many white southerners, who were beginning to lose their traditional Democratic loyalties as the Democrats became the party promoting civil rights through federal action. In the eyes of many voters, problems of crime and disorder in the nation's cities were tied to race. The 'silent majority' (Nixon's memorable phrase) was deeply concerned by the disorder that plagued many major American cities in the late 1960s and early 1970s. By calling for action to ensure that order was maintained, conservatives tied together their concern about crime with worries about race. This law and order message became a dominant strain in American conservatism for the next forty years (Flamm 2005).

Nixon's appeals to the 'silent majority' also signalled the openness of the Republican Party to social conservatism. Conservative intellectuals and the movement around them were open to religious arguments and concerned with social virtue. This intellectual potential was actualized in the early 1970s as a number of grass-roots conservative movements emerged in opposition to social change. The liberalization of abortion laws and the Equal Rights Amendments were the changes that motivated these groups the most, but schooling and gay rights also ignited local contention from time to time. These movements emerged at the grass-roots level in reaction to concern that the traditional values (alternatively, the family values) of the man and woman on the street were under attack by liberal elites. All of these grass-roots movements also had strong ties to different religious communities.

Despite their considerable commonalities, it would not be until the late 1970s that these different social conservative groups would join together to support the Republican Party. Their 1980 success will be examined in the next chapter, but it is worth noting that they voiced, even if often more stridently, a set of concerns that had been circulating among other conservatives for some time. Their fairly direct importing of religious belief into political practice did not cause other conservatives much concern. Social conservative mobilization would – as at the 1976 and 1980 Republican conventions – face opposition from liberal Republicans, which was by that time a much weaker group in the party than the conservative bloc taken together.

The largest of these grass-roots networks was the pro-life movement, which emerged in reaction to the Supreme Court's *Roe v. Wade* decision on abortion in 1973.[10] The abortion issue had surfaced at the state level during the late 1960s as some states began to pass laws that decriminalized the procedure. Debate at the state level was largely an elite affair framed in public health terms, without a great deal of public involvement.[11] Nixon had used the issue in 1968 and 1972 as part of his campaign to detach Catholic voters from the Democratic Party but, as it was an issue decided at the state level before *Roe v. Wade*, there was little in the way of a national movement or pro-life organization before 1973.[12] *Roe v. Wade*, which effectively overturned most existing abortion laws at the state level, initiated a strong popular backlash. It made abortion a national issue and encouraged mobilization on both sides of the question. While initially heavily Roman Catholic in composition, the movement became more religiously ecumenical as many Evangelical, Fundamentalist, and Pentecostal Christians came to see abortion as the major moral issue facing America.[13] Opponents of expanded abortion rights pursued several different strategies at the national level after the Supreme Court's decision. Some tried to ensure that Medicare and Medicaid could not be used to pay for the procedure. Others tried to pass restrictive laws at the state level that would meet the requirements of *Roe v. Wade*. Others – such as the Catholic bishops' conference – focused on initiating a constitutional amendment in Congress that could undercut the legal reasoning behind the decision.[14] Finally, some activists campaigned within both parties (but most successfully within the Republicans) to make a pro-life stance party policy. Social conservatives succeeded in this goal at the 1976 Republican convention. Their success at this convention, as at the conventions that followed, can be attributed to their ability to mobilize a very dedicated cadre of activists who had access to considerable organizational resources in an environment where their arguments from religion and tradition readily gained traction. The success of these activists has made a pro-life position on abortion a critical litmus test for Republican presidential candidates and – in many areas – for Republicans aspiring to lower offices ever since.

Pro-life activism provided the long-term grounding for social conservatism, but the anti – Equal Rights Amendment movement was more immediately noticeable (and ecumenical). Between them, the two largest anti-ERA organizations (Phyllis Schlafly's STOP-ERA and the Women Who Want to Be Women) mobilized many women who had never before been politically involved. While the leadership in these organizations tended to be Republican, they pursued a non-partisan strategy at the state level to stop the ratification of the Amendment. These groups were opposed to what they saw as the feminist attack on women's traditional roles and privileges. As Brown points out, 'the real threat of the ERA was not the specifics of unisex washrooms or drafting women . . . but the broader threat of government interference with the right of families to raise their children in ways prescribed by their religion' (Brown 2002, 16) and a 'concern that America was being destroyed from within by a decline in moral standards' (Brown 2002, 81). In their state-level activism, anti-ERA organizations identified these fears and put forward what was already a common theme among conservatives: that ordinary, grass-roots people could combine to halt the changes foisted upon them by a distant liberal elite.[15]

Two other issues emerged in the 1970s whose impact at the time is hard to determine, but which certainly helped mobilize social conservatives. Opposition to gay rights did not generate a single set of leaders or a coherent national campaign in the 1970s, but successes by gay rights activists often led to local counter-mobilization, such as Anita Bryant's 1974 anti-gay campaign in Dade County, Florida, or the Brigg's proposition in California. While conservatives saw the growing social and political acceptance of homosexuality as very problematic, it was not until the AIDS epidemic of the 1980s and wider debates in 1990s about gays in the military and same-sex marriage that gay rights became a focus for social conservatives.

Social conservatives were also motivated by federal efforts in 1978 to ensure racial desegregation in private schools by removing tax-exempt status from those schools that did not have a percentage of minority students proportionate to the size of the minority population in their area. This proposed change threatened the existence of a large number of private Christian schools, especially in the south. The Carter administration's efforts convinced many that they could not even withdraw their children from the public school system, for 'secular humanists' would even seek to deny them the ability to educate their children in a manner of their choosing.

The emergence of these issues paralleled important changes in the willingness and ability of evangelical Christians to get involved in politics. Since the Scopes trial of 1925, most evangelical, fundamentalist, and Pentecostal Christians had avoided political involvement. Instead, they channelled their energies into building a separate Christian subculture. It included a sizeable network of Christian schools and institutions of higher education, a large print media industry, and a rapidly growing network of churches. It also, thanks to changes in broadcasting laws, grew to include large electronic media ministries. In the late 1970s and early 1980s the most prominent figures in this network were televangelists Oral Roberts, Jerry Falwell, and Pat Robertson.[16]

These groups were strongest in the southern states, which had been solidly Democratic since the Civil War. Naturally, when evangelicals became politically active again during the 1970s, many supported the Democratic Party, especially when Jimmy Carter ran as an openly evangelical candidate in 1976. However, they soon became dissatisfied with the relatively progressive agenda of Carter's administration on civil rights and feminism, as well as with the Internal Revenue Service's proposed changes to the tax treatment of private Christian schools. Disappointed by Carter, evangelical Christians did not retreat back into isolationism. Instead, they swung to the partisan right. They integrated their networks with those of the established conservative movement and worked in support of Ronald Reagan in 1980. The recruitment of televangelists Jerry Falwell and Bob Billings by New Right leaders Richard Viguerie and Paul Weyrich in 1978 is usually taken to mark the emergence of the Christian Right. Organizations like Christian Voice, the Moral Majority, the National Christian Action Coalition, and the Religious Roundtable all set out to use the religious media networks for political mobilization and activity and did so with considerable success during the early 1980s.

Conclusion

The various social conservative groups of the late 1970s took specific positions on the basis of a principle that many other American conservatives had long shared but had not emphasized. Social conservatives brought a new style to politics, placed a novel emphasis on social issues, and emphasized religion more than other conservatives did, but there was nothing in the ideological composition of American conservatism that ruled these positions out of bounds. Those active inside the Republican Party had the support of the conservative movement as well as a rapidly growing base of financial and grass-roots support inside the party. Reagan's 1980 win – as well as successes in the Congress and Senate – showed the Republicans that the 'silent majority' did indeed exist and that it was conservative in terms of fiscal, social, and foreign policy matters. The Republicans have used this formula successfully in the thirty years since, generally integrating social conservatives into their base along the lines prefigured by the conservative thinkers and politicians of the 1960s and 1970s. It was Ronald Reagan's successful 1980 campaign that wove all of these strands together into a sunny and electorally appealing package. Reagan's presidency, as well as that of his successor George H.W. Bush, cemented the place of social conservatives in the Republican Party.

3 Ronald Reagan, George H.W. Bush, and Social Conservatism

Introduction .

During the early and mid-1970s social conservative activists organized themselves in grass-roots social movements that often had ties to the Republican Party, but which almost as often had links to conservative Democrats (especially in the South). Abortion and the Equal Rights Amendment to the constitution (ERA) were their major concerns, though questions about education and the extension of gay rights were episodically prominent. These reasons for action were reinforced by a general dissatisfaction with Jimmy Carter's administration. Carter's 1976 campaign had emphasized his Baptist faith, attracting many evangelical Protestants to his cause. By allowing the IRS to re-examine the charitable status of private Christian schools and by supporting a White House Conference on Families that prominently included feminists and lesbians, Carter soon seemed less Christian to many voters and activists. In addition, the economic problems and foreign policy reverses that many blamed on Carter gave even more reasons for conservative-leaning Democrats (especially in the south) to vote Republican (Moen 1992, Busch 2005).

The dissatisfaction with Carter was part of a wider feeling that American politics and society generally were headed in the wrong direction during the 1970s. Within the Republican Party, this dissatisfaction aided the growth of the conservative part of the party, brought formerly Democratic voters and activists into the party, and eventually guaranteed Ronald Reagan's presidential nomination and landslide electoral victories. Outside of the party, this dissatisfaction saw the existing conservative movement grow as it was joined by two new groups: the New Right, a network of lobbyists and direct mail organizations, and the Religious Right, a set of organizations that mobilized conservative Protestants. There was real potential for these groups to be integrated into the existing Republican-conservative coalition, but it took Reagan's presidential campaign to actualize the process.

After Reagan's 1980 election victory, conservatives of all stripes were excited by the prospects of being able to implement the changes that they desired. On foreign policy and, in some ways, fiscal policy, they succeeded. Reagan led the United States into a much more confrontational stance against the Soviet Union and dramatically increased military spending. This move was paired with a sizeable tax cut that supply-side economists in the administration hoped would actually increase government revenue by encouraging dramatic economic growth. Their theory turned out to be mistaken and resulted in huge deficits. Reagan had promised to balance the federal budget but, faced with the choice between cutting spending, reversing his tax cuts, or running deficits, he chose to run deficits (Cannon 2000). Despite his failure to balance the budget, Reagan did manage to shift domestic policy in a conservative direction. These changes required a significant expenditure of presidential political capital. Social conservatives received significant symbolic recognition from Reagan and other leading Republicans during his presidency, but actual policy changes in their favour were minor and tended to be carried out at lower levels of the bureaucracy, suggesting the important point that social conservatives were recognized as members of the conservative coalition who made important contributions to Republican success but should be considered junior partners in an administration that focused on fiscal and foreign policy.

Reagan's successor, George H.W. Bush, was never the favourite of conservatives that Reagan had been. He had an especially difficult relationship with social conservatives and faced challenges during both the 1988 and 1992 primary campaigns from candidates with whom they had closer links. In some important areas, though, Bush seems to have been as willing as Reagan to acknowledge social conservative concerns. While neither Reagan nor Bush gave social conservatives all (or even much) of what they wanted, twelve years of recognition by the leadership of the Republican Party, combined with significant success by social conservatives at infiltrating the state and local organizations of the party, cemented the alliance between social conservatives, other parts of the conservative movement, and the Republican Party.

The Social Conservative Movement during the Reagan-Bush Era

During the Reagan and Bush presidencies, this integration took place through the development of close links at the level of national leadership between social conservative movement organizations and the party elite. During the early 1990s, the form of this integration changed so that party and movement were closely linked at the membership level. Importantly, though, this was a change in form more than content, for the recognition that the Republican Party granted to social conservatives in policy terms and at election time has changed remarkably little since 1980.

However, the close links between the leadership of socially conservative movements and the Republican Party did accomplish the almost wholesale transformation of social conservatism into a Republican enterprise. This integration was paralleled by the similar integration of feminists and gay rights activists into the core of the Democratic Party. A good part of the polarization around social issues can be attributed to the electoral incentives facing the parties themselves. It is also the result of the integration of social movements into existing party structures, a change made easier on the right as postwar conservative ideology always had an opening for the sorts of concerns voiced by social conservatives. The emergence of the New Right and the Religious Right between 1976 and 1980 focused on turning this potential into actual political power.

The New Right existed before the Religious Right, and, while members of the New Right often made socially conservative claims, it was generally secular in orientation and lobbied on a wide range of issues. It originated in the mid-1970s with a group of conservative activists and fund-raisers who felt that conservatives had paid insufficient attention to political organization and the translation of their ideas into policy. As one of the most important leaders of the New Right described its contribution to American conservatism,

> the Old Right had emphasized the economic issues and anti-communism while the New Right added social issues to the mix, but there really wasn't much outright *disagreement* between the two groups on issues. Their key differences were in temperament and operational style – in short, they

implemented different types of activism . . . the New Right was younger, more impatient, and more aggressive, or proactive. For them the goal was winning campaigns and gaining power . . . the Old Right took a rather lackadaisical approach toward political organizing, while the New Right planned and organized at a feverish pace. (Viguerie and Franke 2004, 127; italics in original)

The two most visible New Right activists, Paul Weyrich and Richard Viguerie, each spearheaded a different approach to making conservative organizations more effective. Supported by the money of the Coors brewing family, Weyrich set himself the task of building a right-wing network of activists and think tanks in Washington centred on his Committee for a Free Congress. Weyrich greatly improved the conservative capacity to lobby Congressional leaders and generate policy proposals (Crawford 1980). Just as important were the fund-raising efforts of his collaborator Richard Viguerie, who used then-innovative computer-controlled direct mail technology to raise money for conservative organizations through large numbers of small donations rather than through a few large donors. This gave the New Right a sizeable advantage over other political groups because post-Watergate changes to campaign finance laws limited the size of individual political donations to parties and candidates (Peele 1984).

It is important to emphasize two features of the New Right's organization. First, the primary loyalty of its leadership was to conservatism, not to the Republican Party. Indeed, Viguerie had made a serious effort to win the presidential nomination of the American Independent Party in 1976 when he – and the New Right leadership in general – despaired of their chances to influence the Republicans. After this, the movement refocused its efforts on the Republican Party and, during the elections of 1978 and 1980, put significant support behind the campaigns of conservative Senate and House challengers (Crawford 1980). Second, the New Right was a fairly short-lived phenomenon that had largely disappeared by 1984. In the late 1970s and early 1980s it was well-funded and influential, but its success at moving the Republican mainstream to the right diminished the need for distinctive organizations promoting a conservative agenda and it was badly hurt by business setbacks that key New Right leaders – most notably Richard Viguerie – suffered during the early 1980s (Peele 1990).

The longest-lasting contribution of the New Right was its integration of social conservatives into the broader conservative alliance both by making social conservatism a core part of its appeals and by reaching out to emerging evangelical and fundamentalist organizations (the Religious Right). The organization of evangelicals and fundamentalist Protestants as a political force came at the end of a period of political quiescence on their part that had begun during the 1920s with the Scopes trial over the teaching of evolution in public schools. The legalization of abortion, a general sense that public education was accelerating moral decay, and court decisions about education and charitable status that eroded the ability of religious Americans to create separate spheres of life for themselves all contributed to this new involvement. At the root of these problems, for members of the Religious Right, was a

> godless society that had replaced firm moral standards with a system of relativism . . . Underlying the challenges to orthodox Christian values, some leaders of the movement argued, was a doctrine called 'secular humanism' . . . Although definitions of that concept varied from one critic to another, social conservatives generally agreed that at its core lay a belief in the supremacy of humanity rather than of God. According to the advocates of traditional social values, the doctrine of secular humanism had become entrenched in the government, schools, media, and other institutions that molded public perceptions. (Wald and Calhoun-Brown 2007, 213)

Over time, those mobilized by this message would make up about one-quarter of the delegates to the Republican national convention and control the Republican Party organization in eighteen states (Wald and Calhoun Brown 2007, 239). To assume that this power was in play from the beginning of their mobilization is, however, to confuse the end of the story with its beginning. Rather, the electoral possibilities were only potential and the organizational forms by which voters could be mobilized were immature in the 1980s. What was present was the notion that these were voters and issues to which Republicans could legitimately appeal in a direct way.

The Moral Majority, Christian Voice, and the Religious Roundtable were the most prominent early expressions of this sentiment. Each tried to convince religious voters that they ought to support the Republican Party. Jerry Falwell, Robert Grant and Richard Zone, and Ed McAteer (the respective leaders of these groups) built on extensive contacts in different sectors of the evangelical community to build up these organizations.[1] The Moral Majority drew on independent Baptist and fundamentalist churches, Christian Voice on Pentecostals, and the Religious

Roundtable on the Southern Baptist convention. While each made efforts to reach outside their denominational bases, none was successful at mobilizing Catholics, Jews, or mainline Protestants.[2]

Until after the 1980 election, these groups were quite dependent on the advice of New Right activists. Paul Weyrich's advocacy of political mobilization by believers was an especially crucial catalyst for the founding of these groups. He is even credited with creating the name of its most visible single organization, the Moral Majority (Oldfield 1996, 101). Weyrich and other New Right activists had the knowledge about Washington and the ties to Republican elites that religious groups needed if they were to be politically effective. Once the religious groups gained Washington experience, they soon surpassed their tutors. This was not merely a result of the large numbers of Pentecostal and Evangelical Christians motivated by religious appeals, but also of the substantial organizational capacities of Religious Right organizations. Each of the three major organizations could boast ties to Christian media networks, extensive networks of pastors linked to the national leadership, and considerable autonomous fund-raising ability.

After the 1980 elections, the leaders of these religious groups claimed credit for the Republican victory and celebrated it as marking a return to family values in America. Their claim of electoral influence was overstated – Reagan's victory over Carter was heavily determined by the state of the economy and large enough that the support of the Religious Right was not necessary to it (Hunt 1981) – but their activism on behalf of the Republican Party, along with the sort of appeals the party had made during the campaign, seemed to mark a turn in American political discourse (White 1991). What they believed to have been their success at influencing the outcome, and the seeming ease with which a sitting president adopted their agenda, profoundly encouraged Religious Right leaders in their belief that, by defending family values and religion, they spoke for the silent majority.

By the time of the 1984 presidential elections, the New Right had largely disappeared as a distinct movement (though some of its leaders remained politically active). The Religious Right was more resilient, but was less decisive in its intervention in 1984 than it had been in 1980. In part, this was because its intervention was expected and was in support of the sitting president (Hunt 1985). It was also due to the capturing of the Religious Right by the party. On some key issues – judicial appointments for example – leaders like Jerry Falwell agreed to simply support 'their' president, rather than criticize his selection of moderate

Republicans unlikely to do much to address their concerns (Moen 1989). Many social conservatives later rejected this uncritical attitude, which has been attributed to political inexperience but also to the fact that, having thrown its support so decidedly behind the Republican Party, the Religious Right had nowhere else to turn (Wilcox 2000).

By 1987 both the Religious Right and the televangelists who provided its most visible leadership were in serious trouble. The Bakker and Swaggert sex scandals discredited televangelists, and the resulting decline in contributions forced major figures like Jerry Falwell to focus more on their preaching and less on politics. The Moral Majority was shut down officially by 1987, by which time most of the other major organizations of the first wave of the Christian Right had been reduced to letterhead status (Moen 1992). At the time, some predicted that these problems meant the end of the Religious Right as a political force in the United States (Bruce 1988). Instead, the decline of the first generation of Religious Right organizations triggered a change in actors and in strategy that was marked by Pat Robertson's 1988 campaign for the Republican presidential nomination. That campaign itself can be taken as the last example of social conservatives trying to influence the party by effecting a direct transformation at the national leadership level. After his defeat in the nomination contest, Robertson changed his strategy and used the organization that he had built up during the campaign as the basis for the Christian Coalition, the organization that replaced the Moral Majority as the most prominent organization of the Religious Right.[3] The Christian Coalition marked a distinct change from the Religious Right groups of the 1980s, for its 'rhetorical appeals [were] more moderate sounding; the issues appeals [were] more broad based . . . and the new organization ha[d] buil[t] impressive grassroots networks' (Rozell 1997, 237).[4] Led initially by Robertson, and then by Ralph Reed, the Christian Coalition launched what Reed referred to as stealth campaigns to promote socially conservative candidates at all levels of politics. The Coalition's prominence did not last past Reed's departure from the organization in 1997, but it did play a critical role in melding the grass roots of the Republican Party and the Religious Right (Micklethwait and Wooldridge 2004, Oldfield 1996). In its focus on influencing the political grass roots, the Christian Coalition marked an important change in the relationship between social conservatives and the Republican Party, the results of which only became fully apparent in the mid-1990s (Oldfield 1996, Watson 1997).

While the New Right and the Religious Right were the most prominent social conservative actors during the 1980s, it is important not to underestimate the role other groups played in mobilizing social conservatives. The pro-life movement, in particular, was a powerful force. Court cases like *Webster* (in 1989) and *Casey* (in 1992) kept pro-life activists engaged and mobilized. Reagan's rhetorical support for them and his administration's occasional pro-life policy interventions (like the Mexico City initiative) provided them with encouragement.[5] While the single-issue pro-life groups continued to be officially non-partisan, they developed closer and closer ties to the Republican Party (Brown 2006). This was because of the Republican's move to the right on social issues and the increasingly consistent pro-choice stance taken by the Democrats.

In ways somewhat analogous to the situation of the New Right, the Republican Party's acceptance of the pro-lifers' concerns make it difficult to talk about the distinctive influence of a single pro-life movement on the Republican Party. In part, this was because of the success of the movement and the New Right at encouraging the convergence on a pro-life position by Republican office holders. In part, it was because the rhetoric of the Reagan administration on abortion outstripped the policy change it was willing to implement. Finally, the movement itself became somewhat fractured during this period due to the growth of new groups (especially the Protestant Religious Right) and substantial disagreements over strategy. Violent anti-abortion protests provoked the most visible disagreement, but a more fundamental one was that between the Roman Catholic hierarchy and organizations close to it that saw abortion in terms of a 'seamless garment of life' that also forced them to call for nuclear disarmament and an end to capital punishment and those groups, often predominantly Protestant, that were conservatives first and pro-life activists second.

The late 1980s and early 1990s also saw a change in the issues that most concerned social conservative activists. After the Equal Rights Amendment to the constitution lapsed in 1982, the issue of formally entrenching equal rights for women in the constitution faded rapidly in importance. Instead, social conservatives were increasingly concerned by the growing acceptance of homosexuality. The set of questions tied up with the recognition of homosexuality had been the subject of episodic, often local or state, conflict during the 1970s. Such issues were thrust into the political limelight by the HIV/AIDS epidemic of the mid-1980s.

Ronald Reagan's Candidacy and Presidency

The emergence of the Religious Right and the New Right did much to mobilize voters for the Republicans. As these voters were often leaning Republican anyway, the real importance of these social movements was that they permanently placed social issues onto the Republican Party's agenda. This change was most visible and important at the presidential level, where rhetoric about traditional values and highly visible linkages with social conservatives became staples of Republican presidential politics. Central to this transformation was the presidency of Ronald Reagan.[6] Despite his popularity with social conservatives, it would be a mistake to see Reagan as unequivocally one of them. His roots in the party pre-dated the emergence of social conservatism, and his own views on social issues were not very conservative. Even on abortion, perhaps the issue on which he came the closest to the social conservative point of view, Reagan had a mixed record. As governor of California, he had signed into law in 1969 one of the country's most permissive abortion laws. It was only after this, according to Reagan, that he changed his mind and declared himself pro-life (Busch 2005). Reagan's own ideology put him closer to laissez-faire conservatives than social conservatives. He was primarily committed to strong anti-Communism initiatives abroad and a firm defence of the free market at home. What Reagan did offer social conservatives was the recognition that they had a place in the Republican Party. Rhetorically, Reagan's campaigns can be summarized in his famous comment to a Dallas meeting of the Religious Roundtable in August 1980: 'You can't endorse me, but I endorse you' (cited in Martin 1996, 217). Similarly, Reagan's call for a 'Morning in America' was easily tied into social conservative rhetoric about rejuvenating family life (White 1990). He also developed public relationships with prominent Religious Right leaders like Jerry Falwell.

While Reagan clearly reached out to social conservatives, he was more concerned with ensuring that the fiscal and foreign policy conservatives he was close to received a prominent place in the Republican Party and in his administration. Reagan's choice of George Bush as his vice-president, for example, upset many of Reagan's social conservative supporters. Social conservatives perceived Bush to be an eastern establishment Republican who was too soft on key issues like abortion. Reagan's response was to make it plain to the social conservatives that he was satisfied with Bush and that party unity was more important than ideological purity. At the same time, Reagan made it clear to Bush that support for the pro-life and anti-ERA planks in the Republican platform was essential to the latter's nomination as vice-president (Greene 2000). Among Reagan's senior staff and cabinet, no one who could be described as an avowed social conservative was to be found (Cannon 2000).

Reagan, and the leadership of the Republican National Committee, entered the 1980 platform process focused on economic and foreign policy issues (Malbin 1981). Social issues, they felt, were too divisive and would not reach out to the working-class Democrats and white-collar suburbanites they hoped to attract. Party activists had other ideas, so the committees charged with drafting the party's position on social issues quickly became contentious. Abortion was an especially delicate topic. In 1976, the party had taken a pro-life stance by positioning itself as the party that takes 'a position on abortion that values human life' within the series of positions it took of concern to families (Republican Party Platform 1976). Pro-choice groups found this too strong a stance and hoped to see the recognition of a woman's right to choose in 1980. Pro-life Republicans, most of whom were Reagan supporters, found the language of 1976 too weak. Both sides in the debate mobilized prior to the 1980 convention through their respective single-issue groups. The subcommittee charged with dealing with abortion was made up of activists from both sides but eventually came to the conclusion that social conservatives wanted and that would broadly define the Republican position until the present day:

> There can be no doubt that the question of abortion, despite the complex nature of its various issues, is ultimately concerned with the equality of rights under the law. While we recognize differing views on this question among Americans in general – and in our own party – we affirm our support of a constitutional amendment to restore protection of the right to life for unborn children. We also support the Congressional efforts to restrict the use of taxpayers' dollars for abortion. We protest the Supreme Court's intrusion into the family structure through its denial of the parents' obligation and right to guide their minor children. (Republican Party Platform 1980)

Also an issue in 1980, though not later in Reagan's presidency, was the Equal Rights Amendment. While opponents of both abortion and the amendment were social conservatives, there were important differences between the activists concerned with each at the 1980 convention. Many pro-lifers at the 1980 Republican convention would have been moderate to liberal Democrats had it not been for a sense that they could accomplish more on abortion by working through the Republicans than through the Democrats. Those opposed to the ERA were otherwise conservative Republicans comfortable with taking right-wing stances on economic and foreign policy issues as well as on social issues (Malbin 1981).

Those delegates trying to preserve Republican support for the ERA (which went back to the 1940s) represented most of the leading female figures in the party. However, Republican feminists were unable to mobilize the same number of convention delegates as their conservative opponents. Reagan himself had quietly promoted a position that would see a platform plank calling for the party to support a number of specific pieces of legislation meant to promote gender equality, but to take a states' rights position on the ERA. However, he and his staff put so little effort into making this position public that committee staff neglected to signal his support of such an amendment when it did come up. The end result was a plank that stated:

> We acknowledge the legitimate efforts of those who support or oppose ratification of the Equal Rights Amendment. We reaffirm our Party's historic commitment to equal rights and equality for women . . . We oppose any move which would give the federal government more power over families. Ratification of the Equal Rights Amendment is now in the hands of state legislatures, and the issues of time extension and rescission are in the courts. The states have a constitutional right to accept or reject a constitutional amendment without federal interference or pressure. (Republican Party Platform 1980)

Though the platform then goes on to support the needs of women in the workforce, the inclusion of language that the party 'reaffirm[s] our belief in the traditional role and values of the family in our society' made it clear to many Republican feminists that their position was no longer supported by the party (Republican Party Platform 1980). It also revealed that the party was willing to take clearly socially conservative stances on two important issues.

Having won the Republican nomination and put together a platform that pleased both the candidate and most of the party, the Republicans and Reagan were well organized for the 1980 presidential race. In Jimmy Carter they faced an unpopular Democrat who was blamed for poor economic performance and some significant problems in American foreign policy – most notably the hostage crisis in Iran. Both parties focused the economy during the election. The Democrats argued that the Republican Party's economic policies would hurt the working class and that Reagan would create a trigger-happy foreign policy; the Republicans blamed Carter for the recession and the decline of American prestige abroad (see Hunt 1981, Busch 2005). Reagan made some significant early appearances – most notably at the Dallas meeting discussed above – that identified him with the Religious Right and stressed his commitment to family values. His appearances making specific links to the Religious Right diminished as the campaign went on. They were replaced by his sunny, but generic, promises to renew America and strengthen families (White 1990).

The 1984 presidential campaign was run on a similar pattern – social conservatives were fairly prominent at the Republican nominating convention but were displaced, at least in the rhetoric of Reagan and most leading Republicans, by a focus on economic recovery and foreign policy considerations as the campaign progressed. The prominence given social conservatives at the convention, importantly, was remarkably uncontested by more liberal elements in the party. As Pomper (1985) explains, this was because the party had become almost exclusively conservative in ideological terms, and so each part of the conservative coalition got its time in the limelight. The rump of the liberal Republican faction could protest the party's movement to the right, but the only significant tension at the convention concerned who from among the Reagan wing of the party would lead it in the 1988 election.

Between elections, Reagan did give important signs of support to social conservatives, especially on the topic of abortion. Concern about this issue was the single strongest motivator for social conservatives during the Reagan presidency. Reagan had insisted in 1980 that his initially pro-choice vice-president clearly signal a pro-life position (Greene 2000). In 1984 Reagan published *Abortion and the Conscience of the Nation*, a book that made the standard social conservative arguments against abortion. He also made it a practice to address, albeit by television feed rather than in person, the annual March for Life in Washington. These symbolic shows of support for the movement were very important. They gave it legitimacy and engendered a strong (and lasting) loyalty to Reagan amongst pro-life activists.

The Reagan administration's record on implementing pro-life policy change was much more limited. Most notably, Reagan did not make the opinions of prospective Supreme Court justices on *Roe v. Wade*

central to his selection of judicial nominees, as social conservatives demanded. Reagan's first appointment to the Supreme Court, Sandra Day
O'Connor, was a moderate on the abortion question. Reagan appointed
her over the protests of Religious Right leaders such as Jerry Falwell
in 1981. Antonia Scalia, his second appointment, was a conservative
on abortion as well as just about every other issue that might come
before the courts. After the Senate's defeat of vocally conservative and
pro-life nominee Robert Bork in 1987, Reagan's last appointment to the
court, Anthony Kennedy, was an ideological moderate. Kennedy and
O'Connor both generally upheld the principles of Roe, even if occasionally allowing some state limitations on abortion rights. Probably more
effective were efforts by Reagan appointees to limit abortions through
bureaucratic means (Blanchard 1994). The Surgeon-General, Secretary
of Health and Human Services, and head of the Office of Personnel
Management – all prominent pro-lifers before their appointments –
did everything within their discretion to limit the number of abortions
that the federal government paid for and limited the type of family
planning programs that federal money would support. However,
such efforts did not require Reagan to spend much political capital in
their support and he seems to have done little to direct their efforts
(Devine 2006).

Abortion continued to be the central concern of social conservatives
during the 1980s, but a new issue, lesbian and gay rights, replaced feminism (as symbolized by the ERA) as the second major concern of social
conservatives towards the end of the decade. While the modern gay
rights movement had begun in 1969 with the Stonewall riots, gay rights
became a mainstream topic of political discussion during the HIV/
AIDS epidemic of the 1980s (Rayside 1998). Federal reaction to the
epidemic caused consternation among social conservatives.[7] Reagan's
Surgeon-General C. Everett Koop, widely respected on the right for his
opposition to abortion, worked to encourage sex education as the best
way to combat the disease. For several prominent social conservatives
such education amounted to a government endorsement of both homosexuality and pre-marital sex and was therefore unacceptable. Reagan,
though, continued to show strong support for Koop throughout the
controversy even if the president himself was extremely slow to address the epidemic (Koop 1991).

Given the focus of Christian Right organizations on influencing the
presidency during the 1980s, it is perhaps not surprising that the situation of social conservatives at the lower levels of the party was more

mixed (Wilcox 2006). Certainly, socially conservative senators like Jesse Helms and Orrin Hatch repeatedly introduced legislation (consistently defeated in both cases) to restrict access to abortion and, in the process, became heroes to social conservatives (Link 2008). As Layman (2001) and Adams (1997) have pointed out, this period saw a convergence to the pro-life position among Republicans in both the House and the Senate. As Koopman argues in his study of the House Republicans, social conservatives preferred to follow the president's lead on social issues and wielded less influence than their numbers would suggest (1996, 103). Socially conservative members of Congress enjoyed few links with movement conservatives and seemed to come by their views as a result of southern political culture rather than as a result of activist lobbying from the emergent social conservative movement (Moen 1989, 1992).

At the state level, the effort to defeat the ERA depended on Republican representatives, though anti-ERA groups often also often gained support from conservative Democrats (Mansbridge 1987). The focus of the ERA's opponents on state-level parties was something of an exception during the 1980s. The period did see some social conservative activism in state and local-level Republican parties – as with the mobilization of pro-life delegates to the national convention in 1980 – but such activism did not become significant or generalized until the Bush era, when activists mobilized by the Christian Coalition made this level of party organization the target of their efforts (Wilcox 2000; Green, Rozell, and Wilcox 2003).

Social Conservatives and the Republican Party, 1988–1992

George H.W. Bush, Reagan's vice-president, was not strongly ideological and did not have a very good relationship with conservatives in the Republican Party. While he had been a Congressman from Texas, his east coast roots, Episcopalian faith, elite upbringing, and long career in Washington made many on the right distrust him. His conservative credentials were especially weak on social issues – he did not make much of his religious beliefs and, until pushed by Reagan in 1980, had been pro-choice. Bush did, though, have extensive foreign policy experience, a reputation as a party loyalist, the trust of moderates in the party, and Reagan's endorsement. This was not enough to calm the fears of some on the right that Bush was too liberal to be trusted, so Bush chose Dan Quayle as his running mate and had his evangelical son, George W. Bush, act as a personal emissary to the Religious Right. Neither strategy made worried conservatives fond of Bush, but he did manage to convince many of them that he was the candidate closest to them who was also likely to win the 1988 election for the Republicans (Greene 2000).

Other social conservatives decided that a candidate of their own was the best guarantee that their concerns would be addressed (Greene 2000). This resulted in the most significant example of social conservative over-reach in American politics: the candidacy of Pat Robertson in the 1988 Republican primaries.[8] Robertson, a Pentecostal televangelist, had stayed aloof from the earlier efforts to mobilize religious voters, on the grounds that the ministry and not politics was the proper place of the clergy. He had a change of heart in the mid-1980s and entered the race for the Republican nomination in the fall of 1986. He ran a straightforward conservative campaign that emphasized his social conservatism and Pentecostal religious beliefs and that was rooted in the Pentecostal Christians who watched his television network. In this regard, its appeal was limited, for other Christians, even other Evangelical Christians, were suspicious both of Pentecostals and of Robertson. As a result, much social conservative support splintered to other candidates like Bob Dole, Jack Kemp, or even Bush himself (who ultimately received Falwell's endorsement) (Oldfield 1996). Moreover, Robertson's appeal was limited because all the major contenders were officially pro-life, opposed the Equal Rights Amendment, and favoured allowing prayer in schools – a sign of how integral to the Republican Party social conservatism had become during the 1980s. The other candidates varied greatly in the importance they attached to such issues, but the rhetorical espousal of social conservatism by all played against Robertson's attempt to use those issues to define his campaign. After some initial successes in states that selected delegates through a caucus process, Robertson lost the nomination quite dramatically to Bush.

Robertson's candidacy was unsuccessful, but it led to some important changes in how social conservatives organized themselves in the United States. Robertson had concentrated his efforts on controlling the Republican Party organization in those states that selected delegates for the national convention through caucuses rather than through primaries. This strategy made sense because he had sizeable numbers of committed activists but only a limited ability to reach beyond this base. This attention to the details of local campaigning inside the party marked a real change for social conservatives, who had previously tended to ignore state and local organizations in favour of building strong relationships between movement leaders and the presidential candidate. It laid the groundwork for the Christian Coalition, which would continue this strategy of mobilizing activists to take over the party's grass-roots organizations for most of the next decade.

After Bush's super-Tuesday successes in the southern states, it did not take long for Robertson and the other major challengers (Jack Kemp and Bob Dole) to drop out of the campaign. Bush easily defeated a weak Democratic challenge in the general election. Facing Democrat majorities in Congress, Bush's domestic agenda seemed to be one of holding the course on the innovations of the Reagan years – incremental changes on education and environmental policy and, above all else, a promise of 'no new taxes.' Abroad, the expectation was that Bush would take a more measured approach to the Soviet Union than Reagan, who alternated between declaring it an evil empire and observing that he and Gorbachev had ended the Cold War.

The unity that the Republicans had been able to put together during the campaign around this incremental agenda did not last very long. Indeed, the Bush presidency saw significant cracks develop in the conservative coalition. It would be difficult to place the blame for this at Bush's door. Rather, a series of events during his presidency posed significant challenges to the terms on which conservatives built their coalition, leading, in turn, to considerable controversy over what it meant to be conservative. Most important, Bush oversaw the peaceful ending of the Cold War. This was a real success, but it also removed the one point on which all conservatives had previously been able to agree: that the Communist threat demanded a significant role for the United States abroad. Within the conservative movement, bitter battles erupted between neoconservatives, who argued for an interventionist foreign policy, and paleo-conservatives, who demanded a more protectionist and isolationist stance (see Frum 1994 and Gottfried 1993 for these respective positions). The resulting debates over foreign policy became most heated with the North American Free Trade Agreement (NAFTA), with many conservatives arguing that the threat to American jobs from cheaper labour in Mexico was too great to allow the agreement to pass. Conservative concern over NAFTA was crucial to the 1992 presidential candidacy of right-wing populist Ross Perot, as well as Pat Buchanan's 1992 challenge to Bush for the Republican nomination (Pomper 1993, Ceasar and Busch 1993). Military interventions – most notably in Panama and Iraq – were less controversial but did consume much of the administration's time and energy. The domestic popularity that Bush's leadership garnered during the Persian Gulf War did not last long; by the end of 1991, it had been replaced by deep dissatisfaction with his handling of the economy.

Another problem for conservatives was Bush's tax increase of 1991. Facing a deadlock with Congress that would have brought the federal government to a halt, Bush acquiesced to demands from the Democratic majority there for an increase in taxes. Even though the need to raise taxes was directly linked to Reagan's inability to reduce spending, conservatives were deeply upset by Bush's reneging on his campaign promise that taxes would not be increased, and the measure passed through Congress with little Republican support. The tax increases were taken as further evidence by conservatives that Bush was not really a conservative and could not be fully trusted at the same time that Bush's own desire to balance the budget severely restricted the domestic initiatives that he could pursue.

On social issues, Bush proved willing to veto any congressional motion that would extend access to abortion (Greene 2000). Moreover, one of Bush's two Supreme Court appointments went to Clarence Thomas, a justice who was conservative on just about all fronts, but was especially critical of *Roe v. Wade*. Despite this appointment, Bush's popularity among pro-lifers never increased. Instead, during his presidency new battles over abortion break out as court decisions, especially *Webster v. Reproductive Health Services*, re-energized both sides of the debate. *Webster* was seen by many as an opportunity for the Republican-appointed majority on the Supreme Court to overturn *Roe v. Wade* (Blanchard 1994). This the court declined to do. The decision gave states more room to restrict abortion than they had previously had but explicitly upheld the basic logic of the 1973 decision.[9]

Nowhere were the tensions in the Republican Party and among conservatives more apparent than at the 1992 Republican presidential convention (Frum 1994). While Bush won the nomination of the party handily, social conservatives played a far more vocal role at the convention than they ever had before. Most observers credit the prominence given to social conservatives at the convention to a deliberate decision on the part of the Bush team to recognize and mobilize them (Frum 1994, Oldfield 1996). This resulted in a platform that continued the party's opposition to abortion and made more of its opposition to gay rights than previous conventions had. The convention also saw some inflammatory speeches by prominent conservatives – most notably Pat

Buchanan's declaration that the United States was in the middle of a 'culture war' (Oldfield 1996). For most voters, however, a weakening U.S. economy was the major issue. Facing Perot's populist challenge, an excellent Democrat campaign led by Bill Clinton, and the absence of key contributors to Bush's 1988 success from the campaign team, the Republicans lost the White House to a Democratic campaign that focused on voter's economic concerns.

The divisions in conservative ideology and the contention at the Dallas convention found echoes in the party's grass roots during this period. Struggles broke out in state party organizations between social conservatives – in general organized by the Christian Coalition – and party activists more interested in fiscal policy, foreign policy, or simply winning office. There is considerable diversity in the outcomes of these debates, but by 1994 the Christian Right was perceived to have a strong position in eighteen state parties and to be of moderate influence in thirteen more (Conger and Green 2002). The period also saw a strengthening of the socially conservative wing of the party in Congress.

This integration of social conservatives into the party's grass roots had important implications, for it cemented the relationship between social conservatives and the Republican Party. The often divisive struggles that accompanied this change did raise questions about how acceptable social conservatism was to Republicans in general. As Green, Rozell, and Wilcox (2003, 15) observe, opposition to social conservatives at the state level

> appeared in three guises. Many Republican activists held more liberal or moderate religious views, reflecting mainline Protestant backgrounds and higher levels of education. Other Republicans were libertarians, opposing government regulation in both economic and social realms. And important elements of the business community were opposed to the Religious Right.

Green, Rozell, and Wilcox also found that the Religious Right and social conservatives were divided among themselves. Case studies of state-level activism point out that many of the struggles between different Republican factions were characterized by a 'professional' versus 'amateur' element in addition to ideological differences: established groups in the party wanted to ensure electoral success, which entailed moderating ideological claims, while social conservatives wanted ideological purity. In some states – like Virginia – experience caused social conservatives to moderate their stance during the 1990s and, as a result, they became an important but not divisive party faction (Rozell and Wilcox 2003). In other states, such as Kansas, a continued insistence on ideological purity by social conservatives resulted in continued conflict within the party (Cigler, Joslyn, and Loomis 2003). While it is difficult to generalize across all fifty states, the increase in the influence of social conservatives in state parties during the 1990s suggests that the first outcome was more common.

Conclusion

The Reagan and Bush years were important ones in the development of American conservatism. During this time social conservatism changed from being a movement, parts of which had a history of being aligned with the Republicans and parts of which did not, to being an integral part of the Republican Party. Social conservatives shared in the general success of the conservative coalition, though the payoff for them was more often in the coin of symbolism than that of policy change. One source of conservative success during both Reagan's campaign and his administration was the conservative coalition was reasonably unified. While social conservatives occasionally criticized the administration for not being aggressive enough on abortion, they were generally satisfied with Reagan's pursuit of 'Morning in America' and his conservative views on foreign policy and the welfare state.

George H.W. Bush's presidency saw significant cracks develop in this coalition, ironically because conservatives had achieved several of their most important shared goals. Foreign policy, which had long been a point of agreement for all conservatives, led to deep divisions among them after the fall of the Soviet Union removed the primary Communist threat. President Bush's fiscal policies, especially his tax increase, were not warmly received by conservatives but did find favour among moderates in the party. Finally, the candidacy of Pat Robertson in 1988 and the militancy that social conservatives displayed at the 1992 convention suggested that social issues could be a critical fault line in the party even a decade after their sudden emergence on the political scene in 1980.

These multiple fractures were no more than a momentary crisis in the alliance between social conservatives, other conservatives, and the Republican Party. By 1994, conservatives had regained ground by organizing a revolution in Congress that established the Congressional

Republicans as a bastion of conservatism and as the majority party in Congress. The 1990s would also see the grass roots of the conservative movement, including social conservative organizations, merge with the regular Republican Party. This did not mean the disappearance of autonomous social conservative organizations – for example, Focus on the Family would become a major player during this period – but it did entail a significant shift in their activities and laid the groundwork for a series of successful campaigns in the later 1990s and 2000s.

4 Social Conservatism and the Republican Party from 1993 to the Present

Introduction

George H.W. Bush's loss of the 1992 presidential election was a low point for American conservatives. It was the first time since 1980 that they did not have a friendly president in the White House, and they were internally divided over foreign, economic, and social policy. The winner of the 1992 presidential election, Bill Clinton, embodied many of the trends that they opposed in American politics. So bad did the situation seem that conservatives began debating if their moment had passed and whether the movement should simply disband (Frum 1994). Social conservatives were blamed by some Republicans both for making the party seem too extreme to succeed electorally and for distracting it from the central issue of the economy. Between 1992 and 1994 electoral defeat and the changed political landscape (especially the end of the Cold War) seemed to support this sense of crisis. The recovery of the conservative movement began in 1994, when the Republicans formed a majority in the House of Representatives for the first time in half a century and also won a majority in the Senate. This 'Republican Revolution' focused mostly on fiscal matters and Congressional tactics, but it renewed the party, helped conservatives see past their ideological differences, and presented a brighter future than conservatives had anticipated only two years before. In 2000, when George W. Bush was elected president, he made much of his links to social conservatives and to the Religious Right. They, in turn, were his most loyal supporters. While Bush was innovative in how he approached many problems, the coalition he led followed to a great extent the lines set down by Reagan a generation earlier: an optimism that the use of American military power abroad could further democracy, a commitment to lower taxes and smaller government that ultimately caused large budget deficits, and a rhetorical commitment to social conservatism.

Underlying these electoral successes and ideological continuity was a shift in the form of the relationship between social conservatives and the Republican Party. During the 1980s, social conservatives were most active in independent social movements that mobilized voters and tried to influence the Republican Party by influencing the party's leadership. After about 1988, with the Christian Coalition providing much of the impetus, social conservatives shifted more of their energy to work within the party so as to influence whichever Republican leader, at whatever level, seemed best able to help their cause. Organizations like the Christian Coalition (until 1997), Focus on the Family, Family Research Council, and the Concerned Women of America continued the tradition of social movement organization begun by the Moral Majority and other organizations. However, the balance of activist involvement shifted, as social conservatives directed more of their organizational energies to the grass roots of the Republican Party (Wilcox 2006).

The power of social conservatism in the Republican Party, as well as George W. Bush's personal commitment to it, are sometimes overstated. It would be a mistake to see either the party or the administration as dominated by 'theocons' as some (Linker 2006) have maintained; the major policy changes of the Bush years (the war on terror and the major tax cuts of his first term) stand in contrast to the far more limited policy gains that social conservatives made while he was president. However, these limited policy gains, when combined with significant rhetorical recognition, do mark the Bush administration as the high-water mark to date of social conservative influence in the Republican party.

Social Conservative Social Movements during the 1990s and 2000s

As we saw in the last chapter, social conservatives had initially mobilized in organizations that tried to influence the Republican Party at the level of its national leadership. During the late 1980s, the first wave of these organizations imploded. Some argued that their passing was a clear sign that social conservatism would soon disappear from the American landscape (Bruce 1988). Such judgments were clearly mistaken. Rather, the Moral Majority and other first-generation Religious Right groups were simply one possible way to organize certain deep-seated sentiments in the population. The specifics of how those who held these sentiments organized themselves politically could, and did, change without altering the central fact of their presence in American politics.

Indeed, the Moral Majority's place as the flagship of American social conservatism was soon taken by another organization, the Christian Coalition.[1] Founded by Pat Robertson after his failed attempt to win the Republican presidential nomination in 1988, this group defined much of social conservatism and Religious Right activism until the late 1990s. While groups before it had caused dramatic change by the attention they drew to social conservative causes, the Christian Coalition was important because it pioneered what proved to be a more effective way for social conservatives to influence the Republican Party. Rather than trying to influence the national leadership of the Republican Party directly, Robertson and Ralph Reed (the organization's director) sought to facilitate grass-roots activism. By building networks of activists to run for positions in local government, on school boards, and for positions in the lower levels of the Republican Party organization, Robertson and Reed believed that they could build a longer-lasting and more powerful political presence than the first-generation groups had. They hoped that these networks would be not only efficient mobilizers of social conservative activists but also training grounds where the next generation of activists could grow in political sophistication.

Reed argued that social conservatives ought to moderate their demands so as to contribute electorally and to build better bridges to other groups in the party (Martin 1996). Somewhat contradictorily, he also advocated 'stealth campaigning,' which aimed to hit opponents before they knew that his group was even active in their area. To do this, Christian Coalition activists concentrated on low-turnout contests, often hiding their affiliation with the organization while encouraging large numbers of activists to become involved in the party. The impressive ability of social conservatives to organize at a grass-roots level made them a formidable force both within the Republican Party organization and – especially in conservative parts of the country – on bodies like school boards. This infiltration of the party's grass roots meant that social conservatives could more successfully influence the party than they had been able to when their focus was directed solely towards the national leadership (Oldfield 1996). As Conger and Green (2002) found, this shift in strategy increased the number of states in which the Christian Right was moderately influential from thirteen in 1994 to twenty-six in 2000, while it continued to be strongly influential in eighteen.

This shift in organizational form occurred at the same time that the issues central to social conservative mobilization changed. Abortion continued to be important at the federal level, especially as the two sides struggled over the partial-birth abortion ban (eventually enacted in 2003 by President Bush), but they had largely fought each other into judicial deadlock by 1992. Sparring over abortion continued at the federal level and could flair up suddenly – when a new Supreme Court justice was nominated, for example – but most pro-life activism moved to the state level after the 1989 *Webster* decision increased the autonomy of states to craft their own abortion laws. The effect of this change has been to defuse contestation over abortion at the national level. As the hot-button issue mobilizing social conservatives at the national level, abortion was largely replaced during the 1990s by questions concerning lesbian and gay rights. Early in the 1990s, the right of gays and lesbians to serve in the military was central to debate. By 1996 same-sex marriage – and other issues connected with the recognition of same-sex relationships – emerged as the central topic over which social conservatives and social progressives battled for the next decade. State ballot initiatives on both of these issues led to a flourishing of smaller-scale social conservative movements and allowed social conservatives to reach out to previously unmobilized voters and to re-energize those activists who had become weary after a generation of struggle over abortion. These local activist organizations enjoyed a mutually beneficial relationship with the Republican Party, especially during the 2004 elections (Wilcox, Merolla, and Beer 2006).

This period also saw the national emergence of new coordinating groups, most notably James Dobson's Focus on the Family. Initially concerned with the distribution of parenting and marriage advice, Focus on the Family had spun off a political lobbying arm (the Family Research Council) in 1983 and had become significantly involved in politics in the mid-1990s. Since then, Dobson and Focus on the Family have become significant political players, especially in voter mobilization efforts and campaigns to constitutionally prohibit same-sex marriage (Gilgoff 2007). None of these organizations, though, defined and channelled social conservative political involvement in the way that the

Moral Majority or Christian Coalition did at the height of their influence; the center of gravity of grass-roots activism had now moved inside the Republican Party (Wilcox 2006, 2002).

Social Conservatives, the Republican Revolution, and the Clinton Administration

Although social conservatives had not been fond of George H.W. Bush, they supported him because he was a Republican who was willing to maintain open communications with them and give them significant recognition, and he was Reagan's declared heir. His defeat at the hands of Bill Clinton was, in part, due to Clinton's successful shifting of attention away from social and foreign policy issues to economic concerns. Clinton's 1992 campaign stressed modest reforms to the programs of the New Deal and an efficient government that could deal with the concerns of the middle class. His slogan 'It's the economy, stupid' tapped into a sense that the economic policies of Reagan and Bush had done little to help ordinary Americans. While he positioned himself on the progressive side of social issues, he did so fairly cautiously and did not make such commitments the focus of his campaigns in either 1992 or 1996 (Waddan 2002).

Given Clinton's attempt to downplay divisive social issues, one might have expected his presidency to have seen a lull in the heated struggle between liberals and conservatives in Washington. Such was not to be the case. If anything, Clinton became the target of the hatred that conservatives had once reserved for Communists, and his presidency was marked by heated culture wars. To some extent, the hostility with which the right greeted Clinton can be attributed as much to who he was as to what he did (Coulter 1998). Social conservatives saw him as the representation of all that had gone wrong with American life since the 1960s. Rumours of his extramarital affairs, his admission that he had once tried marijuana (but not inhaled), his anti-military statements in the 1960s, and his apparent efforts to avoid the draft all made him seem to conservatives as unworthy of being president. That his wife departed from the traditional role of a first lady and had kept her own last name until relatively late in their marriage was only further evidence, to many on the right, that the Clintons could not be expected to embody presidential gravitas or to uphold traditional family values in the White House.

While these questions of image were important, Clinton did have real ties to social progressives and did move towards them in some key policy areas. Critically, one of his first acts in office was to overturn the Mexico City doctrine. This was an executive order, initiated by Reagan and renewed by George H.W. Bush, that denied foreign aid funding to groups or programs that promoted or facilitated abortion. Clinton also made a campaign promise to lift the ban on gay men and lesbians from serving in the U.S. military, though he ultimately backed down on this promise in the face of opposition from conservatives in Congress and the military (Rimmerman 1996).

While the 1992 presidential campaign had been hard fought, after 1994 the conflict between Clinton and the Republicans became bitter as the Republican leadership, especially in the House of Representatives, deliberately pursued a conflictual strategy in their relationship with the president.[2] Led by the Speaker of the House, Newt Gingrich, their plan was to lay out a detailed platform that Republicans would follow when elected (the Contract with America) and then, based on that legitimization, force a showdown between the Republican-controlled legislative branch and the Democratic president. The first part of the plan, electoral success in the 1994 House and Senate elections, was successful as the Republicans won control of both Houses of Congress and a majority of state governorships and legislatures. The first part of the Contract's legislative program, concerned mostly with changes to Congressional procedure, was passed on the first day of the session. The Republicans also promised to introduce, within a hundred days of the start of the session, a series of more substantive changes to American government. These included a balanced-budget amendment to the constitution, a line-item veto, an anti-crime measure, an increase in defence spending, the removal of U.S. troops from UN command, an increase in social security payouts, tax cuts for small business, changes to liability laws, and term limits for politicians (United States Congress 1994). Most of these items were passed quickly.

For social conservatives, the Contract included the following items, which were also passed quickly:

3. THE PERSONAL RESPONSIBILITY ACT: Discourage illegitimacy and teen pregnancy by prohibiting welfare to minor mothers and dènying increased AFDC for additional children while on welfare, cut spending for welfare programs, and enact a tough two-years-and-out provision with work requirements to promote individual responsibility.

4. THE FAMILY REINFORCEMENT ACT: Child support enforcement, tax incentives for adoption, strengthening rights of parents in their children's education, stronger child pornography laws, and an elderly

dependent care tax credit to reinforce the central role of families in American society.

5. THE AMERICAN DREAM RESTORATION ACT: A $500 per child tax credit, begin repeal of the marriage tax penalty, and creation of American Dream Savings Accounts to provide middle class tax relief. (United States Congress 1994)

Gingrich had insisted that all parts of the Contract have the support of at least 60 per cent of voters, so it did not deal with gay rights or abortion. Some social conservatives – most notably James Dobson – expressed displeasure at this requirement. Most groups and activists found the strategy in keeping with their attempts to moderate their position and so extended their support (Gilgoff 2007). The Christian Coalition was of this view, though it did try to ameliorate the lack of attention to its core issues by releasing a supplemental 'Contract with the American Family' in 1995. This contract called upon Congress to 'strengthen families and restore common-sense values' (Urofsky and May 1996, 194). It called for more protection of religious liberty in public places, moving control of education funding to the local level, expanding school choice, enacting a parental rights act, changing the tax act to favour families, ending funding to organizations that perform abortions, imposing a partial-birth abortion ban, encouraging private charities, restricting pornography, privatizing the arts, and increasing work and study programs in prisons (Urofsky and May 1996, 192–231).

In the long run, the attempt to use Congressional power to force a conservative agenda on President Clinton was not successful. This became clear when the Congressional Republicans triggered two shut-downs of the federal government (in November 1995 and from December 1995 until mid-January 1996) during a stand-off with the president over the federal budget. They were demanding a reduction in the growth of Medicare, the abolition of three cabinet departments, and a $245 billion tax cut. At a time when voters were increasingly concerned with medical care and social security, the appearance that conservatives preferred cutting taxes to funding such programs undercut the Republicans (Schaller and Rising 2002). With this reversal in 1995–6 the Republican revolution came to an end, and the 1996 presidential campaign saw Clinton defeat Bob Dole handily (Ceasar and Busch 1997).[3] In light of a popular incumbent and the baggage of an aggressive Congressional Republican strategy of the previous two years, this outcome was not too surprising. Two features of Dole's presidential campaign are important illustrations of the status of social conservatives inside the Republican Party at the time. First, major social conservative leaders like Ralph Reed rejected overtures from candidates with closer ties to the movement so as to support the candidate they felt had the most electoral appeal. Most observers take this as an indication of the movement's growing sophistication.[4] At the same time, the 1996 campaign illustrated the limits to that policy of moderation. Though Dole himself had a strong pro-life record, he proposed moderating the party's platform plank on abortion in hopes of attracting voters. This initiative was quickly quashed by social conservative activists, who ensured that the party's now-standard pro-life plank was maintained (Rozell and Wilcox 1997).

Though short-lived, the Congressional Republicans' success forced Clinton to move to the right during his second term. Gone were promises of a national Medicare system and there was presidential celebration over a balanced budget. For social conservatives, this move to the centre by Clinton was less impressive than it was to their more fiscally minded colleagues. After all, they still had a president in office who embodied for them everything that had gone wrong with American public life since the 1960s. This sense was only worsened when the Monica Lewinsky scandal broke. For social conservatives, the notion of the president conducting an extramarital affair in the Oval Office was both a partisan opportunity and a significant insult to American decency.

More important were Clinton's efforts during his first term to lift the ban on gays and lesbians serving in the military.[5] These efforts failed in the face of pressure from both Congress and the military, as Clinton was forced to settle for a 'don't ask, don't tell position' in 1993. This outcome satisfied neither Clinton's progressive supporters, who were hoping for a complete removal of the ban, nor his opponents (within the social conservative movement and in the military) who hoped to see the previous policy of an outright ban maintained. The tempest over gays in the military was followed by the emergence, in a Hawaii court case, of an issue that would grow more and more important to social conservatives in the next decade: same-sex marriage. While the 1993 decision was subsequently overturned, the Hawaii State Supreme Court's ruling in *Baehr* that the state's prohibition of same-sex marriage was unconstitutional unless a compelling public interest in the restriction of marriage to those of the opposite sex could be shown forced the legislature to amend the state constitution to define marriage as solely the preserve of opposite-sex couples.

Hawaii was only the first of an increasing number of state-level fights over the definition of marriage, battles that reached their peak in the early 2000s. Unlike on abortion, where the increased importance of state-level decision making defused tension at the federal level (except around the partial-birth abortion ban), state-level disputes over gay rights helped to fuel federal-level contention. Nationally, social conservatives won an early victory against same-sex marriage when the Republican-dominated Congress passed, and Clinton signed, the Defense of Marriage Act (DOMA) in the spring of 1996. By 1998, twenty-eight states had passed similar laws (Rayside 2008). Although these constituted significant successes for social conservatives, the DOMAs began rather than ended the conflict over gay rights for two reasons: they could be easily changed by future legislatures and they could be overturned by the courts. The permanent solution, in the eyes of social conservatives, was to pass amendments to the state and (ideally) federal constitutions that defined marriage as a heterosexual institution. The call for such amendments did not progress very far under Clinton, but it became a key issue in the 2004 and 2008 election campaigns.

The most visible form of social conservative activism during the late 1990s had been the attacks on President Clinton regarding the Monica Lewinsky scandal and opposition to gay rights. However, movement leaders realized that they needed a positive goal in addition to these two negative ones. They focused on ensuring that a genuinely socially conservative candidate was selected to be the Republican presidential candidate in 2000 (Watson 1997). This goal was achievable because of their success at organizing within the grass roots of the Republican Party throughout the decade. Although they were not strong enough to get one of their own elected, they were certainly strong enough to ensure that whoever won would do so with their support and, having won, would acknowledge his debt to the social conservatives in the party (Wilcox 2000). Social conservative leaders had hopes that this would mean more substantial action on their issues than the symbolic recognition and limited policy gains that they had received under Reagan, Bush, and Gingrich. Given this in the background, a wide field of candidates began to organize for the 2000 nomination contest, most of whom sought the support of socially conservative Republicans.

Social Conservatives and George W. Bush

Leading up to the 2000 election, five Republican candidates – Dan Quayle, Gary Bauer, Pat Buchanan, Alan Keyes, and Steve Forbes – hoped to build successful presidential campaigns on the conservative wing of the party. While each could claim substantial social conservative credentials, conservatives generally and social conservatives in particular preferred George W. Bush because he was seen as the candidate most likely to succeed in the general election who was ideologically close to them (Mayer 2001). Bush's winning of social conservative support was the result of both his talents as a candidate and the continuing shift in attitude of social conservative leaders. In an initial field that included several more conservative candidates, the decision of social conservative leaders and elder statesmen to support Bush was a sign that they were considering questions of electability more carefully than they had previously (Ashbee 2007). This is not to say that Bush did not have a lot to offer social conservatives and the Religious Right. He had been chair of his father's outreach effort to them during the 1988 campaign and worked hard to maintain the relationships he had formed. As governor of Texas, his actions on gay rights, sex education, abortion, and the promotion of healthy families through the welfare system all went some way to address social conservative concerns. At the same time, he rarely took firm public stands and presented his policies to the public in a way that made them appealing to a wide range of voters. During the lead-up to the 2000 campaign, for example, Bush went on record as opposing gay adoption, a recent court ruling forcing the Boy Scouts to accept gay members, and the use of the federal power to lift state sodomy laws. These positions made social conservatives enthusiastic about his candidacy. At the same time, he was willing to appoint some homosexuals to bureaucratic posts and opposed the efforts of some social conservatives to make an issue of John McCain's meeting with the Log Cabin Republicans (a group of openly gay Republicans) (Ashbee 2007).

Bush also benefited from his unprecedented financial backing. Late in the campaign he was simply able to out-spend his only serious challenger, John McCain. Bush also had the party's establishment and partisan loyalists firmly behind him. Aside from a bitterly fought contest in South Carolina, where the open support of the Religious Right was crucial to Bush's win in a very divisive contest, Bush ran as a moderate who was friendly with the conservative base of the party but who also was well positioned to move to the centre during the general election (Schaller and Rising 2002, Crotty 2001).[6]

Bush's challenge in the general election was to express a conservatism that would mobilize the party faithful while attracting swing voters. The part of the Republican campaign that was crafted most carefully to make this appeal was Bush's call for a 'compassionate conservatism,' a phrase orginated by Marvin Olasky (Olasky 2000). In Olasky's account, which was influential inside the Bush campaign, compassionate conservatism meant focusing on problems of poverty and family disruption that conservatives often ignored. The solution to these problems was not only to provide for the basic material needs of the poor, but to build community-government partnerships in which the communities themselves would be able to deal with their challenges. Often such initiatives would involve partnerships with faith-based organizations and would address the spiritual needs that Olasky identified as being at the root of much poverty. This would mean a solution to poverty that was 'assertive . . . basic . . . challenging . . . diverse . . . effective . . . faith-based . . . and gradual' (Olasky 2000, 16–20).

Bush's campaign biography (Bush 1999) is an illuminating illustration of how he integrated these ideas into his overall campaign. He makes much of faith in the book – indeed, it begins by emphasizing the impact a single sermon had on his political career – but it is a faith that emphasizes the therapeutic ability of religion to redeem self-worth rather than a set of theological commitments. He also makes much of family while offering a vision of his own that downplays his elite status and political background. The last chapter aside, much more is made of his ability to build teams and work with others than of conservative principles or goals. To the extent that the biography examines public policy at any length, it focuses on education reform and the eradication of juvenile crime (Bush 1999, 24–35).

While his concern with education and crime is set out in clearly conservative terms, it is only in the last chapter on 'compassionate conservatism' that Bush tries to sort out what being conservative means for him. A compassionate conservative, for Bush,

> believe[s] in the worth and dignity and power of each individual. My philosophy trusts individuals to make the right decisions for their families and communities, and that is far more compassionate than a philosophy that seeks solutions from distant bureaucracies. I am a conservative be-

cause I believe government should be limited and efficient, that it should do a few things and do them well. I am a conservative because I belie[ve] in a strong national defense to keep the peace. I am a conservative because I support free markets and free trade. I am a conservative because I believe government closest to the people governs best. I am a fiscal conservative and a family conservative. And I am a compassionate conservative, because I know my philosophy is optimistic and full of hope for every American.

. . . Government must be limited and focused, but it has an important job within its bounds. Government is too often wasteful and overreaching. But we must correct it and limit it, not disdain it . . . in some cases, the job is best done not by government itself but by directing government resources to neighbourhoods and parents and schools and faith-based institutions that shape values and change lives. (Bush 1999, 235–6)

This way of articulating his commitments showed George W. Bush to be far more in Reagan's mould than Goldwater's. His conservatism was sunny and optimistic, with few rough edges. Throughout the 2000 campaign, Bush tried to maintain this moderate-sounding language as economic and foreign policy issues dominated both candidates' agendas. Social issues and social conservative activism were less important than they had been for some time (Wilcox 2002). The race ended on a sour note when a Supreme Court decision about voting in Florida, not a Bush victory in the popular vote, decided the election's outcome. As the court split between Republican-appointed and Democrat-appointed justices, accusations of partisan decision making were soon being exchanged, turning a close election into one that called core American institutions into question.

Congressional and Senate elections saw similarly close outcomes. In the Senate, Republicans initially had to depend on the vote of Vice-President Dick Cheney to ensure a majority. They lost this majority in May 2001 when Vermont Senator Jim Jeffords crossed to the Democratic side but then regained it after the 2002 mid-term elections. In the House, the Republicans maintained a majority, but by a smaller margin than they had recently enjoyed. The close 2000 election, and the growing public concerns about the economy and the wars in Iraq and Afganistan, meant that the 2004 election was expected to be a highly charged contest. Despite the central place accorded to the war and the economy, the election was marked by unprecedented attention to social issues by both parties and by a network of social movements and interest groups. This was partly the result of a series of court decisions to do with gay rights that brought that issue to the fore. But it was also due to a deliberate strategy on the part of the Republican Party.[7] After the 2000 campaign, Republican strategists pointed to low voter turnout among socially conservative Christians to explain why they won only a minority of the popular vote in the presidential race. The Bush campaign put a great deal of emphasis on ensuring that these voters turned out in 2004. Much of this effort was organizational, as the Republicans devoted an unprecedented amount of effort and money (the Bush campaign was, as usual, very well financed) to turn out friendly voters in swing states (Conley 2005).

It was the heated debate over same-sex marriage, not abortion, that mobilized social conservatives in 2004. The immediate trigger was the ruling of the Massachusetts Supreme Court in November 2003 that found the state's law against same-sex marriage was unconstitutional and would have to be revised to allow same-sex marriage within 180 days. In the background was the *Lawrence v. Texas* judgment of the Supreme Court earlier that year, which had overturned Texas's law against sodomy. The final trigger was the declaration by the mayor of San Francisco that his city would start registering same-sex marriages. In response, social conservatives organized popular initiatives in eleven states to amend state constitutions so as to forbid same-sex marriage. These efforts dovetailed with Republican efforts to increase voter turnout (Campbell and Monson 2007). Bush also made social conservatism more central to his public image in 2004 than he had in 2000. The references to his personal faith continued, but his commitment to traditional marriage and to restricting access to abortion was made more prominent and more use was made of such appeals in narrowcast direct mailings to voters who would be motivated to vote on the issue (Monson and Oliphant 2007). While the precise effects of these appeals to religious and socially conservative voters are unclear, there is no doubt that the Republicans did better in 2004 than in 2000. They clearly won the presidency and increased their majorities in both the House and the Senate. While Bush benefited from social conservative mobilization on same-sex marriage, many social conservatives were not satisfied with his administration's activity on the question after the election. While Bush did oppose same-sex marriage, he did not push Congress to pass the Federal Marriage Amendment to the constitution, which would have enshrined a heterosexual definition of marriage.

The administration argued that, without a court ruling the Clinton-era Defense of Marriage Act to be unconsititutional, a Senate majority in favour of it was impossible (Durham 2006). The administration also argued that, given the unprecedented activity at the state level over the question, the appropriate role for the federal government was to simply respect decisions that the states were making.

The Bush administration also moved in a socially conservative direction on the abortion issue. He spoke often about his desire to promote a 'culture of life' and appointed a number of pro-life stalwarts – most notably Attorney General John Ashcroft – to senior posts in his administration. On his first day in office, Bush promulgated a number of executive orders restricting or eliminating federal support for organizations that funded abortions abroad. These executive orders (often referred to as the Mexico City provisions) had first been passed by Reagan and renewed by George H.W. Bush, but had been reversed by Bill Clinton. Bush's most important act in the abortion debate was his signing of the Partial-Birth Abortion Ban Act in 2003. Similar acts had been vetoed twice by Clinton, so Bush's support was seen as a signal victory by social conservatives. His administration also blocked the Food and Drug Administration's efforts to approve Plan B contraceptives (which many social conservatives saw as abortifacients) (Jelen 2007).

The administration also spoke out on two issues that social conservatives usually see as linked to abortion: stem-cell research and euthanasia. Research involving human stem cells was becoming controversial in the late 1990s as social conservatives were concerned that, since embryos (given the technology of the day) were the best source of stem cells, such research was either benefiting from or encouraging abortions. As a result, many groups called for a ban on the federal funding of such research. In 2001, Bush struck a compromise by allowing federal funding for stem cell research on existing lines of cells but denying it to research that would use new sources of stem cells.

On euthanasia, the flash point was the 2005 Terri Schiavo case. Schiavo had been in what doctors referred to as a persistent vegetative state since 1990. Her husband, Michael Schiavo, petitioned Florida's courts for permission to remove her from life support in 2002, a motion that was contested by her parents. In October 2003, the Florida Supreme Court found in favour of Michael Schiavo, and her feeding tube was removed. At the urging of Florida's governor, Jeb Bush (the president's brother), the state legislature then passed a law permitting the government to order the feeding tube to be reinstated. This law was ruled unconstitutional in 2004 and a U.S. Supreme Court appeal on behalf of the parents was denied in January 2005. A law, which Bush signed at 1 a.m. on 21 March 2005, gave the parents access to federal courts through which to make their appeals. Their appeals did not find a favourable ruling, however, and Ms Schiavo died at the end of March. More than any other episode, the Schiavo case illustrates that Bush was willing to pay a political cost for at least certain socially conservative commitments. The effort to continue life support was not publicly popular, and the actions of the governor, the president, and some Republican members of Congress all came dangerously close to threatening the independence of the judiciary (Jelen 2007).

Bush's initiatives on same-sex marriage and abortion were the natural extension of policies that social conservatives had always hoped for. Social conservatives were more divided on the faith-based initiatives program (Formicola, Segers, and Weber 2002; Black, Koopman, and Ryden 2004). Both Bush and Democratic candidate Al Gore had promoted versions of this idea during the 2000 campaign. Bush, though, was far more enthusiastic about it and was more willing to relax one of the traditional restrictions on such programs, that proselytizing not be mixed with social service provision. The president was unable to get his enabling legislation passed despite two attempts. Eventually, he implemented a limited version of the faith-based initiatives through executive order. These programs faced substantial criticism from two camps. Liberal groups like Americans for the Separation of Church and State opposed the initiatives for giving religion too much influence in public policy making. Many conservative religious leaders, on the other hand, were suspicious because they believed that government funding would inevitably lead to greater government control over their organizations (Land 2006). Many social conservatives, though, saw the faith-based initiative as a real opportunity to replace the secular assumptions of the welfare state with more fulfilling spiritual ones.

In his nominations to the Supreme Court Bush gave the most to his socially conservative supporters. Because of the Supreme Court's role in deciding issues like abortion and gay rights, social conservatives felt that it was on the appointment of justices that the president ought to listen to them the most. They were especially concerned because two of Reagan's three appointees to the bench proved to be moderates on abortion and other social issues (Ashbee 2007, Krasniunas and Rossotti 2007). Bush's first appointee, John Roberts, met with social conservative approval. When a second position opened with the death of Chief

Justice William Rehnquist in September 2005, Bush nominated Roberts for Chief Justice and Harriet Miers for the open associate seat. Miers was widely seen as unqualified and her nomination was quickly withdrawn. Bush's next nominee, Samuel Alito, came with no such baggage, and social conservatives worked hard to support his nomination. Bush's two appointees seem to have fulfilled the hopes that social conservatives placed in them, most notably by upholding the partial-birth abortion ban in *Gonzales v. Carhart.*

These socially conservative policies would not have been possible without the support of House and Senate Republicans. While no longer in the public eye in the same way they had been during the Republican revolution of the mid-1990s, there is little doubt that the Congressional party has become uniformly conservative (Ashbee 2007). This does not mean that some Republican senators and congressmen did not oppose the socially conservative initiatives of the Bush presidency, but that the party in general was remarkably united behind such initiatives. Much of this can be attributed to the success of social conservatives at gaining power at the state and local levels, which, in turn, depended on their ability to mobilize voters to support their issues (Green, Rozell, and Wilcox 2003).

Conclusion

George W. Bush gave more rhetorical recognition of social conservatives and policy changes than any previous president, even Ronald Reagan. This situation was partly the result of Bush's own beliefs and background, but it was facilitated by the substantial inroads that social conservatism had made among Republicans in Congress, who now find themselves (most of the time) the majority party. The success of social conservatives was grounded in their electoral contributions to and organizational integration into the party and the continuing recognition by conservatives and Republicans of the fundamental legitimacy of their concerns. In short, by 2008 the transformation on the American right that had begun with Goldwater in 1964 and that had taken its first lasting steps with Reagan and the Moral Majority in the 1980s had come to fruition. The migration of social conservatives from the periphery of the Republican Party to its centre was aided by other conservatives. Intra-party opposition came, early on, from moderate or liberal Republicans – people who did not identify as conservative on any issue. As conservatives of all stripes took over the Republican

Party, social conservatives were a part of a general movement, not an isolated group of activists struggling against broadly accepted norms. While not the dominant source of party activists or funding, social conservatives provide a considerable part of the activist brawn that has made the Republicans so successful. In return for the wedding of social conservatism to the Republican Party, the party gave them a great deal of recognition.

That is not to say that tensions have never broken out within conservative ranks. Especially during the early 1990s the tensions between different groups of conservatives could be considerable. However, the status of social conservatives as legitimate players was never seriously questioned at the national level during these times of tension. Instead, the differences were over what one might call normal political matters – debates over leadership, electoral strategy, and how much attention to give specific issues. In short, the norm about the appropriate boundary of politics held by American conservatives consistently included those areas of most concern to social conservatives within the ambit of the political.

The emergence of the Tea Party in 2008 and the surprising popularity of Sarah Palin do not seem likely to shift this situation fundamentally. The Tea Party emphasizes small government and nationalist and anti-elite themes that, while perhaps presented with more volume than during the Bush administration, are nevertheless well within the historical boundaries of mainstream American conservatism. Appeals to traditional family values and (especially in the case of Palin) a pro-life stance on abortion are important, but subsidiary, elements in an agenda dominated by anger over the recession, the government bailout of the financial industry, foreign policy failures, and (often) immigration.

Examined as an ideological movement, there is little reason to see the Tea Party as something novel. Indeed, its emergence echoes themes present in the conservative movement in 1980 and 1994. Where it does represent a real contest is within the Republican Party itself: between those conservatives, perhaps because of their long familiarity with power, who have adjusted to the realities of big government and big business, and the Tea Partiers, who, angry at this accommodation, seek stance more in keeping with the ideological commitments that both groups (ostensibly) hold. Understood in this way, the Tea Party does not introduce new themes into American conservatism or change the weighting of social conservatism in its appeals, but instead calls for those appeals to be made in a more dynamic and ideologically consistent way.

As the next three chapters show, this was not the case with their Canadian counterparts. Rather than operating in an environment where their legitimacy was generally recognized, Canadian social conservatives struggled against norms that defined the areas of most concern to them as inappropriate until the mid-1990s. Before then, the Progressive Conservatives' definition of conservative underlay a norm that rendered social conservative mobilization illegitimate. While different in content, the Reform Party's populism similarly limited social conservative success during the initial stages of that party's life. It was not until a series of institutional changes swept away these norms in the late 1990s that social conservatives could mobilize in a manner similar to that of their American counterparts.

5 The Progressive Conservatives and the Boundaries of Politics

Introduction

In the United States, social conservatives enjoyed a favourable environment: the Republican Party organization was porous and open to the influence of social movements and interest groups; large segments of the relatively religious American population were de-aligned from their traditional party allegiance; and conservative ideology was amenable to appeals to religious authority and to a concern with social virtue. While they have suffered setbacks since then, American social conservatives have built on these favourable founding conditions to become a continuing part of conservatism in the United States. While the feminist and gay rights movements in the United States and Canada emerged in similar ways during the late 1960s, the evolution of social conservatism in Canada has been quite different from that in the United States. Canadian conservatism has always been organized around highly disciplined political parties that are relatively impervious to outside influence. As well, the attitudes of Canadians to social issues like abortion and gay rights have tended to be more liberal than those of Americans. Quebec, like the American south, was a key swing area but was and is the most liberal part of Canada on social issues rather than the most conservative. American conservatism was a movement and an ideology that coalesced after the Second World War in a way that allowed room for social conservatives.

Canadian conservatism had an older and better-established history – one with clear roots in John A. Macdonald's conservatives and, before Confederation, in the Toryism of the Family Compact. The Progressive Conservative Party of the 1960s was not exclusively traditionalist – the majority of party members were probably best understood as laissez-faire conservatives – but the echoes remained. Its dual nature meant that the party had to balance a belief in 'collectivism and privilege' with one in 'individualism and freedom' (Christian and Campbell 1974, 76).[1] As Perlin (1980) has pointed out, such balancing was not always easy for the party. Indeed, he found that the party suffered from a 'minority party syndrome' (198) that rendered it vulnerable to internal discord, especially around questions of leadership.[2] What is important, and even exceptional, about social issues is that they were not used as fodder in these often bitter disputes within the party. Instead, the party came to a conclusion on the basis of three features that pushed it to depoliticize social issues: its past problems with religious controversy, British roots, and preference for consensus or brokerage politics.

The Progressive Conservative Party – while it had left behind much of its anti-Catholic tone by the 1960s – was still overwhelmingly Protestant. The mainstream Protestant churches, whose members comprised the majority of Protestants in the country at the time, ranged from ambivalent to cautiously supportive of the liberalization of legislation concerning divorce, homosexuality, and abortion. Moreover, issues of personal sexuality – especially abortion – were seen as particularly Catholic ones of little concern to those not of that faith. The PCs had suffered repeatedly when the party provoked Protestant-Catholic rivalry, such as had broken out over education or during the conscription crises of the First and Second World Wars, and so sought to avoid issues that carried such potentially divisive religious undertones.

While it is easy to overestimate the influence of British conservatism on Canadian conservative ideology, it is nevertheless the case that Canadian conservatives looked to British practice for solutions in a number of areas. Particularly influential in discussions on social issues was the Wolfenden Report of 1957, which drew a clear line between sin and crime when advising that homosexuality be decriminalized in Great Britain. As Jarvis (2005) has ably pointed out, this line of reasoning represented the conclusion of a series of debates in British society and within the Conservative Party of that country over such topics as abortion, gambling, liquor licensing, prostitution, and pornography. These discussions were far more extensive than debates over similar topics in Canada (with the notable exception of that over abortion), and the Conservative Party in the United Kingdom came to the conclusion that a firm line needed to be drawn between private action (sins) and those actions with a clear social implication (crimes). Given the similarities between the British and the Canadian legal systems and the strong affection of Canadian conservatives for British examples, this solution was a powerful example for Canadian conservatives.

Finally, a striking characteristic of the politics of the era was that both the PCs and Liberals operated as brokerage parties. This meant that they downplayed divisive issues so as to place themselves in the middle of the political spectrum. This brokerage strategy was electorally promising and in fundamental agreement with the PC Party's understanding of conservative ideology. As the party's leader, Robert Stanfield, put it in a 1974 memo to his caucus, being conservative meant avoiding the dangers of ideological polarization, valuing a ' tradition of compromise and consensus' and realizing the need to ' serve the whole country and the whole people' (Stanfield 1974).[3]

In the face of progressive movements which declared that 'the personal is the political,' the response of the Progressive Conservative Party can be characterized as 'the personal has not been, and is not now, a suitable topic for partisan organizing.' Issues of sexual morality such as homosexuality, abortion, or divorce were not legitimate grounds for political mobilization or the imposition of party discipline. This norm remained until the collapse of the Progressive Conservative Party in 1993 and changed only when the Reform Party emerged. This is not to say that the PCs did not contain many who were opposed to removing restrictions on abortion or expanding gay rights throughout the period under consideration – it clearly did include some MPs who opposed such changes.[4] While survey evidence on these questions from the 1960s and 1970s is scanty, it also seems fair to surmise that a sizeable proportion of the party's membership and electoral supporters were also opposed to such measures, given the views of the population at large.[5] However, many who held these views also shared the norm that the personal was not political and so were conflicted about how to take their stand. Those few social conservatives who did not share the norm were at a disadvantage in internal debates because their views were seen as illegitimate within the party whenever social issues emerged as topics for debate.

The Emergence of Social Issues in 1968

Social issues emerged as a topic of political debate in Canada with a Joint House of Commons/Senate committee report on divorce law reform in 1967 and with the introduction of an Omnibus Bill to amend the Criminal Code the following year. Along with more than one hundred other changes to the Criminal Code, the bill proposed two revisions that caused substantial debate: decriminalizing homosexuality and allowing hospitals to set up therapeutic abortion committees. This bill can be taken, along with the Royal Commission on the Status of Women, as signalling the start of second-wave feminism in Canada, the beginning of the gay rights movement, and the abortion debate. While the discussion engendered by the bill would have a significant effect on grass-roots political activity in Canada, it was not itself the result of such activity. Rather, it was a coalition of elites – the Canadian Medical Association, the Canadian Bar Association, the major Protestant churches (especially the United Church), and establishment media players like the *Globe and Mail* newspaper – that pressed for legislative change. Notably absent from this coalition were social movements, as neither the feminist nor the gay liberation movements were politically significant in Canada before the mid 1970s. What these elite groups sought was an administrative updating and renewal of laws that, according to them, no longer matched the country's social reality. Progressives did not base their arguments on claims for equal rights but offered them as practical solutions to social ills. They argued that legal changes would eliminate the health dangers to women posed by illegal abortions; resolve the uncertainties faced by those separated from their former spouses and in new common-law relationships but unable to obtain a divorce; and the problems that the criminalization of homosexuality posed for the treatment of what was increasingly seen as a medical condition like alcoholism rather than a crime.

As with social progressives, there was little popular mobilization around issues of social change on the conservative side. Moreover, in the quarters where one would expect the most support for social conservative ideals, there was little to be found. The mainline Protestant churches were generally supportive of the legal changes Pierre Trudeau, first as justice minister and then as prime minister, was introducing. The Canadian Council of Catholic Bishops (CCCB) accepted changes to the divorce law because the Church believed that it was important that the non-Catholic population, which was not subject to religious restrictions on divorce, not be presented with a law they had no reason to obey. The CCCB did present a brief that opposed abortion, but too late in the process to have much impact.[6] There seems to have been no official Catholic position taken on the legal status of homosexuality (Collins 1985, Cuneo 1989). If the Catholic response was muted, it is safe to characterize the evangelical Christian response as non-existent. At this point, not only were Canadian evangelicals a small group, but most, aside from the Aberhart-Manning connection in Alberta, avoided political involvement as being too worldly (Stiller 1997).

Resistance to legislative change, then, was largely restricted to those members of the federal political elite who felt that the changes being introduced by Trudeau were wrong. Those Liberals who felt this way were restrained by the imposition of party discipline by both Pearson and Trudeau. New Democrats seem to have had no reservations in supporting the bill. The MPs of Le Railliement des Créditistes, alternatively, were not at all hesitant to voice their opposition to the changes proposed by Trudeau, and eventually filibustered the bill. Given the party's origins and strength in rural Quebec, it is not surprising that support for the traditional family, as defined by Catholic social teaching, was a crucial part of its platform.

As the major opposition party, the Progressive Conservatives took a different approach than any of the other parties. Rather than imposing party discipline, the PCs allowed a free vote by their members and encouraged the other parties, especially the Liberals, to do the same. The only position on which the PCs seem to have been united was that the bill should be split so that members would be free to vote on those issues which enjoyed more or less unanimous support among all MPs (drunk driving legislation, for example) separately from contentious issues like divorce, abortion, and homosexuality. Otherwise, PC speakers took on both sides of the debate.

What suggests that the party took its stance because of a norm of non-partisanship rather than because of internal division is the absence of these issues from the recollections of those involved in the party during this period. In the House, John Diefenbaker was 'irrevocably opposed to two of its clauses dealing with sex and abortion' on grounds of conscience (Diefenbaker 27 January 1969), but when the time came for a vote, he found that he had to be in Saskatchewan to dedicate a statue of himself (Diefenbaker 18 April 1969).[7] Diefenbaker's three-volume autobiography, ordinarily so eager to condemn his foes in the party, is silent on the Omnibus Bill (Diefenbaker 1977). Stanfield supported the bill's intent, although he was concerned that it was not split up into constituent parts and that it might lead to inequality (Stanfield 25 February 1969). A biography published with his co-operation in 1973 is silent (Stevens 1973), as are the Stanfield papers in the National Archives (MG 32 C21). Heath MacQuarrie (1992), a political scientist and party insider, does not raise the issue in his history of the period. Flora MacDonald, one of the leading progressives in the party, remembers no 'rancorous debate' at the time (MacDonald 2005). Even those who described themselves as social conservatives remember no deep division in the party over the issue (Epp 2005). Moreover, that a party is itself divided on an issue is usually not a reason for it to allow its members to vote freely – Stanfield did not make it a practice to allow free votes for his members on other contentious issues. If usual Canadian practice had been followed, discipline would have been imposed to bring members in line with the leader.[8] However, this is not what happened – there was something particular about these issues that made the imposition of party discipline unseemly.

Another clue to the nature and existence of the norm is how opponents of the changes articulated their position. Most PC pro-lifers opposed abortion on the basis of personal conscience. They did so hesitantly, often anxious to avoid imposing their views on others. The initial response of Eldon Woolliams, the MP for Calgary North and PC House Leader, can be taken as representative. While identifying his own position (pro-life) he goes no further than to call for a free vote on the bill so that all members could vote in accordance with their conscience (Woolliams 23 January 1969). Admittedly, a few Progressive Conservative MPs did see the bill as representing the arrival of a permissive 'Playboy philosophy' (Dinsdale 17 April 1969). Such language would suggest a broader, more encompassing social conservative critique of social change. However, even these MPs agreed that the issue was not a partisan one. This lack of partisanship mirrors the position of those MPs who did support the changes (and they included Robert Stanfield), but who did so hesitantly and kept partisan considerations out of their speeches.

The Omnibus Bill's provision for the decriminalization of homosexuality produced a similar response from PC speakers. One group (which included Stanfield) supported the change, although with reservations about the clarity of its wording. As Stanfield saw it, if 'this sort of conduct involves purely a matter of private judgment [the position of Justice Minister John Turner], then I find that difficult to accept. Surely we recognize that the interests of society are involved with respect to what goes on in private and that the criminal law must regulate such conduct' (Stanfield 25 February 1969). Stanfield's stance points to the confusion that dealing with emerging social issues could create for traditionalists – he argued for the procedural norms of traditionalism (an ordered society) but against the substantive position those norms had embodied (the condemnation of homosexuality).

The next type of argument came from those who argued that, while they did not want the existing law enforced, neither did they want to see homosexuality approved of. This group included some members who rooted their position in their understanding of the traditional practice of Western countries. Most of these speakers (who included Woolliams, the House Leader) portrayed homosexuality as a mental illness requiring treatment, not as a crime deserving prison time.

A final group made the argument that the law should teach morality to the public and that this function required the criminalization of homosexual acts. For this group, even questioning whether homosexuality should be permissible was a sign of social decay (see Dinsdale 17 April 1969, Diefenbaker 18 April 1969). Even these hard-line speakers, though, did not portray homosexuality as an issue paralleling the normal partisan divides.

All three groups drew on British examples and arguments, but these examples seemed to best support those who argued for legalizing abortion, easing restrictions on divorce, and decriminalizing homosexuality. In the United Kingdom, the Wolfenden Report of 1957 had recommended and the Sexual Offences Act of 1967 implemented a loosening of criminal restrictions on homosexuality. The British Abortion Act of 1967 had similarly loosened restrictions on abortion, allowing it up until the twenty-eighth week of gestation, subject to a doctor's approval. Both debates had been resolved after substantial debate and the decision, by the British Conservative Party, that sins were different from crimes (Jarvis 2005).

The overall tendency to keep the personal separate from the private seems in keeping with the vision of conservatism presented by the party's leader, Robert Stanfield, in a 1974 memo to his caucus. It stressed the dangers of ideological polarization, the value of a 'tradition of compromise and consensus' and the need to 'serve the whole country and the whole people' (Stanfield 1974). Such an understanding of conservatism, when applied to a deeply divisive issue, would have militated against pushing the politically hot button of abortion for partisan gain. There is little to suggest that this norm changed during the 1970s. There was, of course, the emergence of a substantial social movement activism around abortion, lesbian and gay rights, and feminism, but the first two issues did not find much room on the agenda of party politics. Trudeau's consistent refusal to reintroduce legislation on abortion rights throughout the 1970s (despite his promise of a free vote on the issue in 1972–4) had much to do with this situation, as did increasingly heated debate on economic and constitutional issues that preoccupied the country's political elite.

Social Movement Activism and Charter Politics

While the 1970s and early 1980s saw little change in how political parties stood on social issues, the period between the implementation of the Omnibus Bill and Brian Mulroney's election in 1984 saw a great increase in social movement activity on these topics. On the progressive part of the political spectrum, this was perhaps the golden age of Canadian feminism (Young 2000). The latter part of the period would see the expansion of Canadian lesbian and gay rights activism (Rayside 1998, Herman 1994, Smith 1999). Initially, social conservative movement opposition to these changes was concentrated in the pro-life movement. It is important to note, however, that it was not until the late 1970s – as the result of an internal power struggle – that Canadian pro-lifers could really come to be described as conservative. During the 1970s, Canada's largest pro-life organization was the Toronto-based Alliance for Life, which, in 1973, spun off a political lobbying arm, Coalition for Life. Both of these organizations had a heavy presence of academics in their respective leaderships and saw abortion as a human rights issue with parallels to the war in Vietnam or the proliferation of nuclear weapons rather than as a threat to the traditional family (Cuneo 1989).[9] These groups' approach to the issue, while affirming the desirability of a much stricter law on abortions, was also to call for the alleviation of the social and economic conditions that placed women in a position where abortion seemed an attractive option.

With the growth of the pro-life movement, this moderate vision became a source of contention between the movement's academic Toronto leadership and its growing grass-roots base of conservative rural Catholics. This base preferred a stricter analysis of the situation that saw abortion as part of a 'contraceptive mentality' that the Liberal government and its feminist allies were promoting to undercut family and religious life (Cuneo 1989). In 1977, this ideological divide split the movement, as members of the grass-roots/moralist group split off and founded Campaign Life. By 1979, Alliance for Life had moved its offices to Winnipeg and more or less imploded, leaving Campaign Life as the organizational face of the Canadian pro-life movement.

Campaign Life's identity, which has been remarkably consistent since its founding, has been to stress that it is a 'life and family movement' (Hughes 2006). Until the late 1990s, the organization's Catholic roots and Ontario base meant that, although officially non-partisan, most of its connections were with the federal Liberal Party. Since then, grass-roots links with the Reform Party and the mobilizing effect of Stockwell Day's leadership campaign moved the organization and many of its supporters towards the Canadian Alliance and then the new Conservative Party. While flexible in its partisan affiliation, Campaign Life's uncompromising commitment to its principles made it a very difficult partner for politicians.

Sometimes equally immoderate in its tone, but with closer ties to the Progressive Conservative grass roots and more religiously mixed than the predominantly Roman Catholic pro-life movement, REAL (Realistic, Equal, Active, for Life) Women of Canada was founded in 1983 to protest abortion and state support for feminist organizations. In the 1990s and 2000s REAL Women focused more and more on gay rights issues. In this way, its program is more broadly socially conservative than those of the pro-life groups, who tend to focus primarily on abortion and intervene only occasionally on gay rights (Foster 2000, Erwin 1993). This group's connection to the PCs was quite strong, but seems to have been mostly at the constituency level. Given its grass-roots character, it is perhaps unsurprising that many of REAL Women's activists left the PCs for the Reform Party during the late 1980s (Foster 2000).

In tone and membership, Campaign Life and REAL Women (and shorter-lived groups like them) defined one face of Canadian social conservatism during the 1980s. They developed substantial memberships and achieved some level of media visibility. At the same time, their stridency made them difficult political allies. Campaign Life, in particular, developed a reputation for being so demanding in what a politician had to do to be considered pro-life that it alienated party members and leaders who might otherwise have been happy to listen to their message (Cuneo 1989). Other, more moderate, groups with socially conservative messages seem to have been better received by Canadian political parties generally and to have enjoyed access to the Mulroney government (Stiller 2005).

In the 1980s, the most organized and effective of these groups was the Evangelical Fellowship of Canada (EFC). Founded in 1964 as an umbrella group for Canadian evangelicals, by 1983 EFC had expanded its activity into political lobbying. Initially headed by Brian Stiller, EFC had a broad policy agenda. It lobbied for increased foreign aid and measures to reduce domestic poverty, in addition to taking conservative stances on issues such as gay rights and abortion. Active on a wide range of issues and aware that it represented only one voice in a diverse society, EFC stressed a pragmatic and incremental approach to social issues. While firmly pro-life, the organization supported Mulroney's attempt to compromise (in Bill C-43) in the hope that its pro-life language could be incrementally expanded to reduce the number of abortions in Canada (Stiller 1997, 2003, 2005; Clemenger 2005).

The Canadian Council of Catholic Bishops (CCCB), the other major Christian institution that took socially conservative positions during Mulroney's tenure, also tried to lobby pragmatically and moderately. Again, this may have been because of the range of stances that the bishops would take – some of them quite progressive on issues like poverty, foreign aid, or war. In addition, like EFC, the bishops were also aware of Canadian diversity and thus hesitant to mandate a particular course of action (Cuneo 1989, Higgins and Letson 1990). Indeed, the moderation of the bishops caused the deepest divide in Canadian social conservatism during the 1980s: that between the Canadian Catholic hierarchy and Catholics in the pro-life movement. While the Canadian Council of Catholic Bishops and bishops individually did lobby on the pro-life side, their refusal to demand protection for the unborn in the Charter or to declare abortion the *only* issue of concern to Catholic voters won them the hostility of the pro-life movement. At the same time, the bishops saw the language and tactics of Campaign Life to be misguided and inflamatory. Toronto's Cardinal Carter, for example, ultimately forbade Campaign Life from distributing literature or holding meetings in Toronto's Catholic parishes and schools (Cuneo 1989).

The EFC and, to a lesser degree, the CCCB had good access to the leadership of the PC Party under Mulroney. While groups such as Campaign Life and REAL Women could put protesters in the streets and sometimes influence events in a particular riding, their stridency greatly reduced their influence with the national leadership in Ottawa. The difference in approach, though, was a real divide in the movement and the cause of considerable tension.

Between 1968 and the emergence of the abortion and gay rights debates of the mid-1980s, Canada's political structure underwent a dramatic change with the passage of 1982's Constitution Act – especially its Charter of Rights and Freedoms. The Charter opened up litigation as a way for activist groups to pursue their goals (Morton 1992, Smith

1999). This made it possible for activists to place their issues firmly onto the political agenda even if political parties found social issues too politically dangerous to handle. Unlike the situation before the introduction of the Charter, social issues could not be kept out of the public spotlight through the inaction of the political parties or the cabinet.

The emergence of the courts and social movements as major actors also produced a significant shift in the terms of the abortion debate. No longer was it understood primarily as a public health or religious issue. Instead, it was a contest between two seemingly irreconcilable rights claims: the right to life of the fetus and the women's right to control her body (Campbell and Pal 1991, Brodie 1992). When court decisions, especially that in *Morgentaler v. the Queen*, put the issue back on the agenda, the NDP was again firmly pro-choice and the Liberals divided. As both the 1988 motion and 1989's Bill C-43 were declared free votes by the government, neither opposition party imposed party discipline.[10] The absence of the Créditistes meant that it was socially conservative PCs who were furthest to the right on the issue. Despite consistent polling evidence that most Canadians would have preferred some kind of middle-ground solution to the issue, court decisions and the level of social movement mobilization made it very difficult for the Progressive Conservatives to find such a position (Tatalovich 1997). As a result, the situation that the Mulroney PCs encountered was far more difficult than that faced by the party under Stanfield. While this difficulty was somewhat moderated by their ability to decide abortion through free votes, it still represented a real problem for the government.

Social movement mobilization in the general population found parallels in the Progressive Conservative Party. Pro-life PCs had formed a caucus to organize themselves after the 1984 election victory,[11] while pro-choice PCs had organized as Tories for Choice in the 1970s. The number of MPs consistently active in these groups was small (weekly attendance at the pro-life caucus was around twelve to fifteen MPs) and they were run mainly by backbench MPs, but they distributed information more broadly and provided the two poles around which MPs grouped themselves on the issue. These two groups seem not to have extended their activities beyond organizing these caucuses. There seems, for example, to have been no effort to contest riding nominations or other party offices on a pro-life/pro-choice basis.

The Mulroney government attempted to address the abortion issue three times. In May 1988, Mulroney introduced a complicated motion that took a gestational approach, with abortions early in pregnancy being subject to fewer restrictions than abortions later in pregnancy. Appended to the main motion, however, were two contradictory amendments – one emphasizing the rights of the fetus and one a woman's right to choose. This failed on procedural grounds, as the House did not grant the unanimous consent this unconventional procedure would require. Then, in July, the government sought the 'sense of the House' by introducing a motion (again embodying a gestational approach) but without the amendments of May. MPs brought a series of amendments forward on the motion, but none passed and the motion failed (Brodie 1992, Flanagan 1997).

After the *Daigle* court case (which found that the fetus had no legal status under existing law), the government decided that it had to introduce a new law. It attempted to do so with C-43 in the summer of 1989. In an attempt at compromise, the bill would criminalize abortion 'unless the abortion is induced by or under the direction of a medical practitioner who is of the opinion that, if the abortion were not induced, the health or life of the female person would likely be threatened' (quoted in Brodie 1992, 98). Unlike the completely free votes on the resolution, on C-43 the government whipped Cabinet ministers in support of its compromise position and passed the bill through the House of Commons 140 to 131 in the face of opposition from both pro-choice and pro-life MPs. Bill C-43 was then defeated in the Senate, in part because two PC senators voted against it (Brodie 1992, Flanagan 1997).

While the cabinet ministers being whipped in support of C-43's middle way made a difference to the vote count, the rhetoric used by pro-life and socially conservative MPs in both 1988 and 1989–90 is similar enough that the debates over the resolution and the bill can be considered together for the purposes of evaluating the party's norms. An examination of the language and strategy of the Mulroney government suggests that it was acting in accordance with the same basic principle as had Stanfield's Tories in 1968: abortion was not an appropriate subject of political mobilization and the party should not define itself by a stance on the issue or permit much internal mobilization on the topic.

On both the resolution and the bill, most pro-life Tories in caucus no longer bookended their comments with observations on the limits of decisions based in personal conscience. Instead, by and large, their position was justified on rights grounds. They also argued that, as a moral issue, abortion was something that created divisions as much within parties as between them (Health Minister Jake Epp's speech was representative of this approach). Approximately a dozen pro-life MPs who spoke took a straightforward social conservative approach to abortion, linking its liberalization to the decline of social mores (Nickerson 26 July 1988; Plourde 26 July 1988).

Even such speakers, however, avoided making the issue a partisan one. Strikingly absent from the debate were pro-life or pro-choice Conservatives who took that position because they were a conservative. MPs stated that they were pro-life because they were fathers (all the pro-life speakers were men), doctors, lawyers, believers in human rights, or Christians, but never because they were Progressive Conservatives. Similarly, PC pro-choice MPs argued for decriminalization, more funding, and women's choice because they were women, because of compassionate reasons, or because they believed that the law was ineffective, but they did not take their position because of party membership. This, as in 1968, stands in contrast to members of other parties who linked their partisan status to their position on the question.

This rhetoric seems to have matched the behaviour of MPs in the caucus room. While members of both the pro-life and pro-choice persuasions organized on the issue, neither those organizational ties nor positions on the issue spilled over into other policy discussions.[12] This tendency was reinforced and encouraged by Mulroney's considerable skills at consensus building. While free votes on abortion certainly helped to diminish the tensions between the two sides, Mulroney's own style of management reinforced the idea that it was not a debate with parallels to other policy areas. As Mulroney put it, in a speech which made no partisan distinctions and echoed the party's 1968 stance, 'what we have been called upon to do, as elected representatives of the people, is to determine under what circumstances the state should characterize abortion not as a sin, but as a crime' (Mulroney 1988).

Social Conservatives and Gay Rights in the 1980s

Until the failure of Bill C-43 in 1990, abortion was the issue of greatest concern to social conservatives in Canada. The 1980s also witnessed the emergence of legal and political moves to extend equal rights to homosexuals. Not as important as abortion during the 1980s, lesbian and gay rights emerged after 1993 as the dominant issue for social conservatives in Canada. Aside from the 1968 Omnibus Bill, contention over gay rights had previously occurred at lower levels in government. Most provinces faced significant pressure to amend their human rights codes to prohibit discrimination based on sexual orientation during the mid- to late 1970s and 1980s. In 1976, Quebec was the first province to prohibit discrimination based on sexual orientation; several other provinces waited until the late 1980s to change their human rights codes. At the municipal level, in Toronto and Montreal, gay rights activists mobilized to oppose police raids on bathhouses in the 1970s and early 1980s, leading to significant mobilization to change police attitudes and behaviour (Rayside 1998, Herman 1994, Smith 1999).

A number of factors prevented much lobbying of legislators on either side of this issue at the federal level during the 1980s. On the part of many gay rights activists, there was a sense that there was little point in lobbying the Tories, especially given the urgent need to deal with the AIDS epidemic. Further, section 15 (the equity rights section) of the Charter came into force in 1985, making litigation a profitable avenue for the advancement of gay rights. The relative inaction at the federal level on the part of lesbian and gay social movement activists was matched by the parallel inactivity of their socially conservative counterparts. While the federal parties were not subject to much lobbying on gay rights during the 1980s, the issue did arise occasionally. However, it seems that, on the occasions when gay issues did make it onto the caucus agenda, neither progressives nor conservatives in the PCs saw them as being of great political importance.[13] The most serious debate over gay rights occurred in 1986, when Justice Minister John Crosbie suggested that the federal human rights code should be amended to include lesbian and gay rights. His proposal was tabled in the face of social conservatives in the caucus (Crosbie 1997). While Crosbie's autobiography decries his 'troglodyte' opponents (Crosbie 1997, 271), in retrospect he does not see the issue as having been vitally important at the time, at least in comparison to the otherwise full government agenda (Crosbie 2006).

In the late 1980s some significant court cases addressed homosexual rights, and a number of provinces addressed discrimination based on sexual orientation in their human rights codes. But it was not until 1992 that the PCs moved on the issue again. In the fall of 1992, Justice Minister Kim Campbell lifted a ban on gays and lesbians in the military in the face of judicial pressure. Then, in December 1992, she introduced an amendment to the Canada Human Rights Code that would have added sexual orientation to the list of reasons private employers could not discriminate against employees. Campbell's description of the negotiations leading to the proposed amendment show the continued importance for PCs of gay issues being excluded from the political agenda. For her and her fellow MPs (even those who opposed the change) the central concern was to ensure that the issue 'fell off the table' (Campbell 1996, 214).

The 1993 election marked the end of the Progressive Conservative Party as a powerful player in federal politics. While it still received a significant part of the popular vote, it never again was a serious contender for office. A victim of Canada's first-past-the-post system, it lost its Quebec seats to the Bloc Québécois and its western seats to the new Reform Party. Its hopes of restoring federalism dashed, and outflanked to the right on economics by the Reform Party (and the Liberals, in many ways), the party was unable to differentiate itself clearly from its competitors during the 1990s. One area where it did manage to redefine itself was on social issues. Particularly during Joe Clark's leadership (1998–2003), the party stressed its progressive position on gay rights. Clark went out of his way to contrast his progressive sensibilities with the socially conservative ideas of Preston Manning and other Reformers. Clark also insured that those social conservatives who had not already left the PCs for Reform or the Canadian Alliance knew that they were not particularly welcome in the party (anonymous interview).

Conclusion

From 1968 until 1991 an important part of the Canadian Progressive Conservative Party's approach to abortion remained consistent: the party rejected the notion that abortion was a partisan issue. Instead, it characterized it as a moral issue necessarily left up to the personal values of its MPs. This norm placed a powerful limit on the arguments available to Canadian social conservatives, for it prevented them (at least publicly) from arguing that their approach was the one that conservatives should take. The party's position on lesbian and gay rights was remarkably similar. While not nearly as contentious during this period as abortion, there seemed to be a general consensus that gay rights issues were something best kept off the political agenda.

This situation helps us understand why social conservatives had such a low profile on the Canadian political landscape before the Reform Party emerged. It is not that they did not exist or that issues of concern to them did not arise, but rather that the implicit norms about the boundaries of politics held by members of the Progressive Conservative Party gave them little room to argue for their position. This norm also seems to have limited the activity of those who were progressively inclined within the party – they too did not desire to make too big a deal of such 'non-political issues.'

The rise of the Reform Party changed this situation in two ways. For the PCs themselves it sent them looking for ways to differentiate themselves from the new party, to argue that they were the genuine embodiment of Canadian conservatism. One of the ways in which they did this was to stress the Progressive part of their title when dealing with social issues. Especially under the leadership of Joe Clark, this strategy allowed them to stress how different they were from Reformers and from American Republicans of the late 1990s. Second, Reform injected a heavy dose of populism into Canadian politics and, generally, caused a re-examination of the institutions and beliefs of Canadian conservatism. Even here, though, social conservatives were limited in their success by a norm that designated social issues as moral ones to be decided upon only through populist mechanisms. Only over time – and for a complex set of reasons including the transition from abortion to gay rights as the most prominent area of contention and a decline in the power of the party's leadership – did the Reform Party came to accept social conservative concerns as legitimate. By the time Reform itself was replaced by the Canadian Alliance, this transformation had progressed to the point where the new party would select a leader who was openly socially conservative and who would include social conservative appeals as a core part of the party's programs.

6 Social Conservatives and the Reform Party of Canada

Introduction

Many western Canadians, especially Albertans, were dissatisfied with Canadian politics in the mid-1980s. The region had a long-standing sense that its concerns were ignored in Ottawa, and a severe economic depression, after the oil boom of the late 1970s, created solid grounds for claims that this lack of political voice was hurting the region's general prospects. Federal economic policies – most notably the National Energy Program – had seemingly exacerbated these problems. The victory of Mulroney's Progressive Conservatives in 1984 raised hopes that these issues would be addressed, but to many westerners the government seemed too focused on Quebec to address their needs. Soon, a series of fringe western independence parties emerged, offering separation as the solution to these problems.

The Reform Party's founding impetus was the desire to solve the west's problems without resort to independence. It was initiated by a group of prominent westerners (most notably Preston Manning, who became the party's leader) who organized a meeting to review solutions to the political problems dogging the west. While they tried to avoid partisan language and presented a range of populist options to the meeting, it seems clear that the formation of a new political party was what Manning and the other organizers had in mind for their first major meeting in May 1987 (Ellis 2005). This Vancouver meeting was followed by a convention in Winnipeg in October that officially launched the new Reform Party of Canada. This convention established a party constitution and a party platform (the *Blue Book*). While the party failed to win a seat in the 1988 general election, success in a by-election a few months later sent Deborah Grey to Ottawa as the first Reform MP. In 1993, the new party swept the west, narrowly missing becoming the official opposition but confirming itself as the most dynamic part of Canadian conservatism. By the late 1990s, dissatisfaction with what seemed the party's perpetual opposition status led to a series of attempts to unite the right; as a result, the Reform Party was absorbed into the Canadian Alliance in 2000 with a new leader, Stockwell Day.

Throughout its existence, the Reform Party struggled to reconcile populism with conservatism. As one of the party's senior officials put it:

> The party that Manning has built has a dual identity. It is partly the trans-ideological populist movement portrayed in his rhetoric, but it is even more a new conservative party formed by a mass migration of voters deserted by the centrist leaders of the Progressive Conservative party. Perhaps the most interesting story . . . lies in the complicated interplay between the leader's unique mystical populism and the quite ordinary conservatism of most Reform supporters. At the time of writing, the identity of the party remains suspended between these two poles, but that is unlikely to go on indefinitely. (Flanagan 1995, 4)

This dual nature meant that the party would sometimes act on conservative principles and sometimes on the basis of what Manning had decided was the popular will. For example, it was committed to balancing the budget but preferred to maintain agricultural subsidies and (as of 1995) shied away from suggesting free-market solutions to the problems of the Canadian health care system. On issues of sexuality and abortion, Flanagan argues, Manning had avoided taking a conservative stance. At least as of the mid-1990s, Manning's 'various statements regarding homosexuality may represent confusion or tacking in the wind, but they are certainly not the utterances of a leader imposing a hard-right agenda on the party' (Flanagan 1995, 15).

Following Ellis (2005), a portrayal of social conservatism in the Reform Party must recognize this ideological tension and the evolution of the party's organization and beliefs over time. On some questions of concern to social conservatives, most notably abortion, the party imposed fairly strict restrictions on their activism and consistently maintained that the topic was a moral one to be settled through popular initiative, not partisan contestation (Foster 2000, Harrison 1995). When challenged, Manning would use his power as leader to enforce compliance on the issue with the agreement of caucus and the party's grass-roots members (Ellis 2005). This position was widely held within the party even though the party's members and leadership were generally pro-life – a compromise held together by a generally held differentiation between ultimate ends and populist procedure.

Abortion was dealt with at the party's founding. Gay rights, the issue through which social conservatives would gain full legitimacy in the party, emerged as a topic for significant debate in the mid-1990s. The party had to come to a position on the issue as it emerged and at the same time as Manning's control of the organization began to fade. Add to this a public divided over gay rights issues (especially the definition of marriage) and an opportunity was created for social conservatives. What is striking is not only that social conservatives managed to gain themselves a place in the Reform Party, but that they have maintained a place for themselves in the more moderate parties that have followed it – the Canadian Alliance and the Conservative Party of Canada. The twelve years of the Reform Party's existence, then, represent a turning point in the history of Canadian conservatism, even if the party was not as unambiguously socially conservative in the way it is sometimes made out to be.

Social Conservatives and the Founding of the Reform Party

Reform's early platforms and announcements stressed four issues: fiscal responsibility, democratic renewal, a Triple-E Senate, and opposition to bilingualism.[1] Notably absent in early party discussions and planning were social issues.[2] The extent of the treatment of social issues in the 1990 *Blue Book* is a statement that the party would 'affirm the value and dignity of the *individual person,* and the importance of strengthening and protecting the *family unit* as essential to the wellbeing of individuals and society' (Reform Party 1990, 26; italics in original). This language certainly did not exclude social conservatives; indeed, it may well have been attractive to them. It stops well short, though, of being an espousal of state intervention to maintain traditional family roles or the definition of those roles through religious authority, which, as we have seen, are two fundamental parts of social conservative ideology.[3]

This principle remained in subsequent versions of the party's platform, but was muted by the party's stance on moral decision-making. Being more specific, this set of guidelines would have far more of an impact in later debates than the above statement. The party's stance on moral decision making is first found in an addition to the 1990 *Blue Book* that stated:

> We believe in freedom of conscience and religion, and the right of Canadians to advocate, without fear of intimidation or suppression, public policies which reflect their most deeply held values.

Abortion

A. The Reform Party commits its Members of Parliament to stating clearly and publicly their personal views and moral beliefs on the question of abortion, to asking their constituents to develop, to express, and to debate their own views on the matter, and to seeking the consensus of the constituency on the issue.

B. In the absence of a national referendum, the Reform Party expects its Members of Parliament to faithfully vote the consensus of the constituency in the appropriate divisions of the House of Commons if such a consensus exists. If such a consensus does not exist or is unclear, Members of Parliament shall vote in accordance with their publicly recorded statements on the issue. (Reform Party 1990, 26)[4]

In comparison to the prominence given to themes of populist reform, regional alienation, or free-market economics, though, the place that social conservatives found early in the party's life was restricted and ambiguous. They were recognized as a constituent part of the party, but there is no indication that the leadership or vast majority of the membership of the party during the years after its founding saw it as a vehicle for social conservative mobilization.[5] It is important to recognize that while its call for populism was a radical departure from the practices of the established parties, it was also an approach that could be very unpopular with social conservatives in general and pro-life activists in particular, who did not trust such mechanisms to give them the results they desired (Flanagan 2005, Jim Hughes 2006). As MacKenzie (2005) has detailed at length with regard to social conservatives in British Columbia, populism – in anything other than situations where it guarantees social conservatives certain victory – is not for them an acceptable solution. As one of the British Columbia pro-life activists interviewed by MacKenzie put it, populist principles created 'nothing more than . . . "a typical power-hungry party without principles"' (2005, 160).

Despite these restrictions, some room was granted to social conservatives within the party's broader populist framework (Flanagan 2005,

Cameron 2005). The mention of healthy families is an important example at the level of principle. Organizationally, socially conservative members of the party were channelled first into the Family Task Force and then, once a Parliamentary caucus was formed, into a Family Caucus (Manning 2005). Both of these groups had responsibility for investigating the impact of government action on Canadian families. Social conservatives were also able to stop the attempt to form a 'women's work group' in 1990, arguing that such a group would simply mirror the organizational feminism of the other parties (Harrison 1995, 213). The party's consistent efforts to appeal to the 'ordinary Canadian,' usually as a member of a heterosexual family, undoubtly helped to appeal to social conservatives as well.

Preston Manning offered the justification for this division most explicitly, sought to transcend left-right distinctions, and to base his politics in the common sense of the common person. He also paid significant attention to the relationship between religion, morality, and politics. He saw two approaches to the problem. One method, which he disapproved of while acknowledging that it could be both effective and popular, was to articulate a specifically Christian political agenda. Such an approach is rooted in Old Testament notions of a godly government and has been pursued by those on both the political right and the political left. However, Manning also argued that a specifically Christian political agenda is unsuitable in a diverse society as it frightens non-Christians with the threat that successful Christian political action might force others to act as if they had Christian beliefs. It also puts Christians into the position of merely being one interest group among many others (Manning 1988).

The alternative, which Manning saw as more appropriate for political action in a diverse country like Canada, was for Christians to cooperate with someone else's political agenda. Accepting their minority status and the idea that God can work through both believers and non-believers, he felt that Christians needed to make a firm distinction between their personal faith commitments and their public political agenda:

> I have a personal agenda as a believer, but it's not a political agenda. It has to do with my own spiritual development and that of my family . . . On my agenda I have a prayer for a spiritual awakening in Canada – I think Canada's never had a spiritual revival in the way that other communities have had. But these are not political items on my personal agenda. (Manning 1988, 13; see also Manning 1992, 2002)[6]

Central to this distinction is the realization that 'committed Christians' are a minority in Canada and so their political strategy must fundamentally be a witnessing one (Manning 1992, 107). If their witness fails to attract minority support, this is simply a cost of being principled. On topics like abortion this would mean that the politician in question would have to resign their office so that their riding could be represented by someone with views closer to the popular sentiment (Manning 1992).

This populist position was not merely a matter of principle for Manning, for he was willing to act quite definitively to ensure that the party presented a populist and moderate image on social issues. Most famously, Manning expelled two MPs – Dave Chatters and Bob Ringma – in 1996 for defending the 'right' of business owners to employ gay employees only at the 'back of the shop.' That an MP who criticized this pair, Jan Brown, resigned before Manning could expel her for breaking party discipline suggests that there were matters of tactics and organizational maintenance at stake as well, but his action was consistent with Manning's actions on other occasions. At the 1988 founding convention, Manning 'lecture[d]' (Ellis 2005, 26) delegates who he believed to be pursuing social conservatism. After the convention, he used the moral issues resolution to 'control radical elements within the party by arguing that any attempt to develop firm policy stances on these issues would be contrary to the spirit of the Abortion Resolution and would hamper MPs in their ability to faithfully represent their constituents, one of Reform's key populist planks' (Ellis 2005, 66–7).

It would be unfair to characterize the party's restrictions on social conservatism as being entirely of Manning's own making, though his stature as leader doubtless did much to solidify the distinction between public and private that the party took. Similar notions were widely held by the party's members and activists as well. For example, at party conventions in the late 1980s and early 1990s, the overwhelmingly pro-life and pro-capital punishment party membership routinely voted to declare that capital punishment and abortion were moral issues best decided by referenda or some other means of expressing the will of the majority, rather than by a parliamentary vote or partisan contest (Ellis 2005). Ellis's analysis of the views of activists who attended the 1992 assembly found that views on abortion, the most prominent social issue of the day, ranked eighth out of eleven factors in influence on the overall views of party activists (2005, 109). And he found that delegates who became party members later in the party's life were more likely to rank abortion as a major issue, suggesting that participants at the 1988 and 1989 assemblies that institutionalized the party's rules on the question were even more likely to see abortion as a relatively unimportant matter than those at later ones. A social conservative effort at the 1992 convention to force the party to take a substantive stance on abortion received a lecture from the chair, Stephen Harper, on appropriate populist methods. Harper's dressing down of social conservatives received a rousing ovation and the support of 95 per cent of the delegates when the motion came up for a vote (Ellis 2005, 133).

From Abortion to Gay Rights

By the mid-1990s the issue that the Reform Party had initially defined as moral – abortion – had moved off the legislative agenda, and so the party's populist position on it was never put to the test.[7] Instead, the delicate definitional distinction made by Reformers between moral and political issues was tested by the topic of gay rights. This shift had some important implications for the nature and organization of Canadian social conservatism outside of party politics, and presented a different strategic situation for the party. Each of these differences between abortion and gay rights meant that the change in topic gave social conservatives more popular support and made their arguments easier to combine with populist appeals.

At the broadest level, the change made the religious nature of the social conservative movement less Roman Catholic by mobilizing evangelical Protestants in sizeable numbers. This is not to say that some evangelicals (or other Protestants, for that matter) had not been opposed to abortion (many were), but many more were mobilized by debates over gay rights. Conversely, Catholics tended to oppose abortion more strongly because they saw it as the graver moral threat. Gay rights were, for many Roman Catholic activists, a significant problem (especially if the definition of marriage was involved) but much less so than open access to abortion.[8] In terms of party politics, the more that the social conservative movement was made up of evangelical Protestants, the more natural was its alliance with right-wing parties (traditionally the parties of Protestants in Canada). Negatively, the increasingly evangelical face of Canadian social conservatives made it easy for their opponents to argue that Canadian social conservatives were simply following the example of their American counterparts (see MacDonald 2006, 2010) – this despite the fact that many prominent evangelical groups, like the Evangelical Fellowship of Canada (EFC), claim to maintain closer ties to their British co-religionists than to their American ones.[9] Somewhat surprisingly, the shift from abortion to gay rights as the central topic of debate did not cause major changes in the social conservative groups involved in litigation and lobbying.

The four major groups reviewed in the last chapter – the Evangelical Fellowship of Canada (EFC), the Canadian Council of Catholic Bishops (CCCB), REAL Women of Canada, and Campaign Life Coalition) – continued to dominate as the long-term core of the movement and maintained their previous strategies and characteristics. They were joined as a major player by Focus on the Family Canada, which was the only major Canadian social conservative group with close ties to the American movement. There also appeared, from time to time, organizations that were little more than letterheads for a particular individual's activities (Malloy 2007) or groups that were active only at the provincial level (MacKenzie 2005). Such organizations did not change the division in the movement between those who favoured a moderate, incremental approach and those who wanted to take a hard-line stand against social progress.

Another important difference between the two issues was that public opinion on abortion had been remarkably stable in Canada since the mid 1970s – a consistent 12–15 per cent of the population opposed it under all circumstances, 50–60 per cent of the population believed it ought to be allowed under certain circumstances, and 25–35 per cent supported a woman's right to choose under any circumstances (Smith and Tatalovich 2003, 260). On gay rights, alternatively, public opinion was more evenly divided and changing rapidly during the 1990s. In 1992, for example, 24 per cent of Canadians supported same-sex marriages and 61 per cent opposed them. By 1998, opinions had changed so that 40 per cent of Canadians supported and 52 per cent opposed same-sex marriages (Smith and Tatalovich 2003, 268). Abortion offered few potential partisan gains for the party, while opposition to gay rights did not carry with it the same disabilities and, in fact, could be seen to offer certain electoral advantages in a situation where the other parties ranged from decidedly undecided (the Liberals) to strongly in favour (the NDP).

Additionally, debates over the substance of gay rights, like the conclusion of the debate over abortion, were closely intermeshed with debates over the proper relationship between the courts and Parliament. As Smith (1999) argues, the opportunities opened by the Charter of Rights and Freedoms made litigation a popular strategy for gay rights groups. To some extent, litigation eclipsed earlier grass-roots mobilization strategies on both sides of the debate. As with abortion, the increased role of the courts caused a consolidation of language as both sides adopted 'rights talk' that meshed with the language of the Charter. The increased role of the courts also gave a powerful reason for populists to agree with social conservatives that progressives were threatening both society's proper structure and Canadian democracy (see Knopf and Morton 2000).

While the increased prominence of the courts adds an important dimension to the gay rights debate, it did not remove the issue from the legislative agenda. Indeed, with a Liberal government in power after 1993, progressive activists felt more confident in calling for change at the federal level than they had during the Mulroney years. Those lobbying the federal government now included a national lobby group, Equality for Gays and Lesbians Everywhere (EGALE) (Smith 1999 and Rayside 1998). While persistently short on resources and without an extensive grass-roots base of its own, EGALE was generally successful at promoting the extension of gay rights in the federal jurisdiction. It did a lot, for instance, to keep Prime Minister Jean Chrétien's 1993 campaign promise to add sexual orientation to the human rights code in front of the public (Rayside 1998, 118–23).

The Reform Party and Gay Rights

Against this backdrop of social movement and court activity, gay rights began to be debated almost immediately after the 1993 election sent a significant number of Reform MPs to Ottawa. The question of gay rights had been a minor campaign issue in that election, as the Liberal Party had suggested it would act on the recommendations of the Human Rights Commission to extend equal treatment to same-sex couples (Rayside 1998). Throughout the 1990s and 2000s, gay rights would replace abortion as the most hotly contested social issue in Canada. The Reform Party responded to this change in two ways, both of which opened up significantly more room for social conservatives inside the party.

Outside of Parliament, party assemblies soon showed that they would oppose gay rights in an unambiguous way that they never opposed abortion. The 1994 Ottawa Assembly passed a resolution that declared the party 'support[ed] limiting the definition of a legal marriage as the union of a woman and a man' (Reform Party 1994). The 1996 Vancouver Assembly passed a similar resolution that the 'family should be defined as those individuals related by the ties of blood, marriage, or adoption. Marriage is the union between a man and a woman as recognized by the state' (Reform Party 1996). These resolutions clearly placed the party on the socially conservative side of the debate over gay rights.

A lengthier example of how the party proposed dealing with gay rights is contained in a 'Draft Statement of Homosexual Rights' that the leadership circulated to party candidates, executive councillors, and regional co-coordinators in September 1993:

> The Reform Party believes in the principles of minimum state intervention in the lives of individuals, that all Canadians should be treated equally under the law, and that all Canadians should be protected from discrimination. The Reform party does not believe in the principle of granting special status or special entitlements in law to any group based on its cultural, linguistic, ethnic, or sexual characteristics. The application of these principles would recognize the right of homosexuals to exercise their freedom of choice in their private lives, and would condemn any instances of 'gay-bashing' or discrimination against homosexuals. We would not support the extension of family benefits to same-sex partners since the rationale for such benefits is generally related to the procreation and raising of children – a rationale which does not generally pertain to homosexual liaisons. (Reform Party 12 September 1993)

The linkage of populism and opposition to gay rights is also apparent in the other way in which the party took a stance on gay rights: the statements of its members in Parliamentary debates. These debates were foreshadowed in 1994, when members of all parties tabled petitions from their constituents arguing for or against the legal recognition of same-sex relationships. In the spring of 1995, a Bloc Québécois member introduced a private member's bill to extend 'legal recognition of same sex spouses' (Ménard 26 April 1995). Because it was a private member's bill, debate was not extensive but did reveal that some Reformers (and the significant number of Liberals who opposed the bill) were willing to make arguments that gave the legal system the role of promoting traditional sexual morality, portrayed the traditional family as the bedrock of society, and warned of Canada's moral decline.

Bill C-33, a government bill to add sexual orientation to the prohibited grounds of discrimination in the Canadian human rights code, was introduced into the House on 29 April 1996. In an effort to assuage critics of the bill within the Liberal Party, the bill included a preamble which stated that nothing in it should be read as affecting the traditional definition of the family then enshrined in common law. Allan Rock, then the justice minister, was especially insistent that the changes to the human rights code would not facilitate the extension of spousal benefits to same-sex couples. With the Bloc, the NDP, and the vast majority of Liberals (of whom only twenty-eight voted 'nay') supporting it, Bill C-33 passed into law by 9 May.

While Liberals like Tom Wappel and Roseanne Skoke took a strong line against the bill, almost all Reform MPs opposed Bill C-33. While party discipline was not imposed on the vote, the forty-five 'no' votes cast by Reform MPs made it seem as if social conservatives dominated the party. While this almost monolithic opposition made clear the party's opposition to the extension of gay rights, a closer examination of the reasons given by the party members reveals the importance of populist, rather than conservative, reasons in their thinking, at least in their public utterances.

One of their arguments – that the law should not seem to condone or promote homosexuality and that tradition should be maintained – was clearly socially conservative. It assigned to the legal system a role in promoting a conservative vision of private virtue and saw the recognition of gay rights as creating a disturbance in society:

> Canada may recover in time from the huge financial mess it is in, but the damage that will be caused to Canadian society by the changes made this week to the Canadian Human Rights Act will haunt us for many generations to come . . . the irreparable harm caused by creating virtually equal status for gay and lesbian marriages with others will take a lot longer to heal. We will destroy the very fabric of our society by allowing the courts to redefine marriage. (Breitkreutz 7 May 1996)

Those who took this view (such as Jay Hill, Lee Morrison, Monte Solberg, Myron Thompson, and John Williams) accepted that previously private matters had become issues for political contestation and sought to ensure that the law articulated a conservative vision of moral behaviour.

The other Reform MPs who opposed the bill did not do so for conservative reasons. They were upset that the change was being forced through the House of Commons by a government without a clear mandate on the question. More deeply, they saw in the recognition of gay rights the extension of differentiated rights to yet another group. Rather, they argued, the legal regime needed to maintain an undifferentiated set of rights that applied to all. Preston Manning and Sharon Hayes (the leader of the family caucus) offered this sort of populist argument.[10]

The Reform Party's position in the 1996 debate was, then, a mixed one. Significant numbers of its MPs did ground their positions in socially conservative principles. Others, though, based their position in populist language about the correct manner in which public policy decisions ought to be made. Equally important, is that Reform MPs and the party's resolutions did not draw explicitly on religious arguments in taking their position, as they would do later in the decade. Since the desirability of religious arguments in the public square is an important aspect of social conservatism, one can see signs in the 1996 debates that social conservatism had not yet been fully recognized on the Canadian right.

The Reform Party's position in the House was overshadowed, and its public image damaged, by a newspaper story that ran on 30 April 1996. The story was based on an interview that Bob Ringma, one of its whips, had given in 1994. In that interview, he stated that he believed an employer should have the right to fire a gay or lesbian employee or move them 'to the back of the shop.' Dave Chatters, an MP from Alberta, then defended Ringma's remarks, while Calgary's Jan Brown began denouncing the 'rednecks' in the party.[11] Ringma's remarks became the centre of political attention for some time. Manning's eventual response illustrates how a powerful leader is able to maintain discipline in a Canadian party: Ringma and Chatters were suspended from the party and Brown resigned before she could be suspended (Manning 2002, Grey 2004, Ellis 2005). Importantly, Manning's heavy-handed action did not receive any criticism from within the party. This is strong evidence that Manning was acting in accordance with the generally held beliefs of party members.

After the passage of C-33, the debate over gay rights in Canada shifted to the question of whether or not same-sex marriages ought to be recognized by the state. Throughout the latter half of the 1990s, MPs of all parties introduced motions or petitions concerning same-sex unions into the House of Commons. However, large-scale debate broke out in reaction to the *Rosenberg* decision of the Ontario Court of Appeal that extended spousal benefits to same-sex couples. Reform MP Eric Lowther introduced a private member's motion that[12]

> in the opinion of this House, federal legislation should not be altered by judicial rulings, as happened in the redefinition of the term 'spouse' in the Rosenberg decision, and that, accordingly, the government should immediately appeal the Rosenberg decision. (8 June 1998)

While *Rosenberg* was a case about the extension of gay rights, most Reform speakers framed their arguments as protests at the power of judges to overrule decisions made by Parliament (Eric Lowther, Grant McNally, Jason Kenney, Erwin Schmidt, and Chuck Strahl 8–9 June 1998). Only a few Reform MPs made the socially conservative argument that 'what is happening here is an abandonment of family values' (Pankiw 8 June 1998) and that 'the institution of marriage and the family unit . . . is the fundamental building block of society' (Vellacott 8 June 1998).

More extensive debate broke out the following year over a motion to define marriage as being only between a man and a woman. Again, Eric Lowther took the lead and framed his motion as a response to 'public debate around recent court decisions, to state that marriage is and should remain the union of one man and one woman to the exclusion of all others' (Lowther 8 June 1999). A few MPs emphasized the position of the traditional family as the basic unit of society (Ken Epp, Erwin Schmidt, Chuck Strahl, and Jay Hill). However, most speaking to the motion emphasized a populist discontent with important decisions being made by the court system, rather than by Parliament (Eric Lowther, Gurmant Grewal, Gary Lunn, Monte Solberg, Maurice Vellacott, Diane Ablonczy, Jim Pankiw). Somewhat surprisingly, Lowther's motion passed the House of Commons with overwhelming support from the Liberals, who – for once – were not subject to party discipline on the question.

On gay rights, unlike abortion, the Reform Party developed a clear position. Its ambiguity on abortion meant some significant tension with the pro-life movement initially (Hughes 2006), but as the debate became more defined in terms of gay rights, the Reform Party became the Canadian party with the most room for social conservative activism. This shift occurred at the same time as, and offset, the transformation of

Reform from an ideologically driven and regionally based third party to a truly national contender for office. This combination, and the shift in norms that accompanied it, meant that Reform was more socially conservative at the end than at the beginning of its life.

This transformation into an office-seeking party had its roots in the early 1990s. This was a period of great success and growth for the party, but it was also a period of increasing debate over what, exactly, were the party's goals. For Manning and much of the leadership, especially after Reform had replaced the Progressive Conservatives as the major right-wing party, the party needed to try to form the government (Flanagan 2005, Manning 2002). For others, located mostly outside the party leadership, the party should continue to be a western party promoting the full version of its populist ideology (Ellis 2005). This tension between those who argued the party should seek office and those who wanted it to articulate policy manifested itself frequently. It underlay debate about whether the party should expand into Ontario in 1991 and, more significantly, about what attitude Reformers should take to those Progressive Conservatives who remained after 1993. For the 1993 and 1997 elections, Reform's plan was based on a two-election strategy: 1993 would see the party displace one of the existing major parties and 1997 would see it form the government. This strategy would require substantial institutional and financial growth for the party (most notably the building of an Ontario organization), but there seems to have been little notion that ideological change would be required to appeal to eastern Canadians. Instead, all the party needed to do was improve its technique and organization (Manning 2002, Flanagan 1995).

The Reform Party, in short, was seeking to form the government while keeping its principles intact. Its leaders were betting that the average Canadian would support them if only those principles were better articulated and the party better organized. After Reform's disappointing performance in the 1997 election, the party's leaders began exploring what more dramatic changes would be necessary if the party was to be able to seriously challenge the Liberals for government. Central to any chance Reform had to win office was a better relationship with the still substantial remnants of the PC Party. The need for cooperation grew clearer after the 1997 election, when the PCs staged a comeback, winning twenty seats, most in Atlantic Canada, and 19 per cent of the popular vote across the country (Woolstencroft 2000, Patten 1999). However, the federal PC leadership (especially Joe Clark) was very resistant to any such cooperation (Segal 1997).

There was real cooperation between federal Reformers and prominent provincial PCs, notably those associated with Alberta's Klein and Ontario's Harris governments. Working together with these groups, Manning launched a proposal for a 'United Alternative' (to the Liberals) at the Reform convention in London, Ontario, in May 1998. Manning rejected the idea of describing the proposed party as conservative. He argued that it could be built around four principles already in Reform's *Blue Book:* fiscal responsibility, social responsibility, democratic accountability, and institutional reform. Most other Reformers, and certainly those PCs involved in the process, saw it as an opportunity to 'unite the right' and finally push the Liberals out of office. After his idea was approved by the Reform convention, Manning then successfully shepherded the idea of a new party through the first United Alternative convention, again in London, in February 1999. This was followed by a second United Alternative convention and a membership vote in the spring of 2000 that formed the Canadian Alliance. As we will see in the next chapter, this new party ended up being conservative rather than populist and with Stockwell Day as its leader, not Preston Manning.

Conclusion

It can be said that the Canadian right became united in 2000 as a result of the Reform Party. This openness to social conservatism represents a major change in Canadian conservatism and one that seems – a decade later – to have become permanent. Part of the reason for this move was the state of public opinion on gay rights, especially on same-sex marriage, during the 1990s. This cannot be the entire story, though, for no other party sought to exploit this opportunity (a substantial portion of Liberal MPs and Cabinet supported the heterosexual definition of marriage on the 1999 vote). Apart from the importance of public opinion, the emergence of social conservatism in Canada should be understood in the context of the dramatic changes that Reform caused on the Canadian right. These changes created both organizational (by transforming how conservatives organized) and normative (by introducing populist, and disrupting Progressive Conservative, notions of conservatism) turmoil. Social conservatism succeeded within Reform on the basis of their opposition to gay rights, in part, because they could link such opposition to both populism and conservatism in a way that pro-lifers had earlier been unable to do. They were also able to make their arguments in an environment where they were not faced with an entrenched previous norm about what the appropriate boundary of politics for conservatives.

The transformation that Reform triggered seems to have become permanent. As the next chapter shows, the fortunes of social conservatives have waxed and waned since Reform passed from the political scene, but they have found a consistent place on the Canadian right. They, and their concerns, are now seen to be part of normal politics, on which the Canadian Alliance and Conservative Party of Canada took clear positions. This situation could not have taken place had the Reform Party not created a situation of organizational and normative flux and had the switch from abortion to gay rights as the dominant social issue not made at least some aspects of social conservatism electorally attractive.

7 Social Conservatives and the Unified Canadian Right

The Reform Party quickly established itself as a force to be reckoned with, but many within the party felt that its growth had stalled by the late 1990s. By splitting right-wing votes with the PCs, Reform was helping to ensure continued Liberal governments, which neither the PCs nor Reformers wanted. Concern with this situation eventually led Preston Manning, other prominent Reformers, and representatives of some provincial PC parties to begin the United Alternative process. This led to the creation of a new party, the Canadian Alliance (CA), in 2000. The new party identified itself as a conservative party, rather than as a populist one, and sought a national, rather than regional, base of support. It had the clear goal of driving the Liberals out of office. Despite these changed goals and ideology, it was mostly composed of former Reformers, for most federal Progressive Conservatives continued to oppose the idea of joining with Reform to form a single party.

Unexpectedly, Alberta Treasurer Stockwell Day defeated Preston Manning in the contest to lead the CA. For many socially conservative activists, Day's openly pro-life stance and proud articulation of his Pentecostal faith made him an attractive figure who might fundamentally change Canadian politics. Day benefited from this source of support, but most of his success was due to his image as a media-savvy politician who would lead the party to victory. Day's leadership was short-lived: he was unsuccessful in the 2000 election, proved to be a poor caucus leader, and was very prone to media gaffes. Perhaps most important, little was done to unify the right under his leadership. These faults led to several senior members of the party leaving to form the Democratic Reform Caucus (DRC) in the spring of 2001. The defection of respected party members like Chuck Strahl and Deborah Grey soon caused a general call for another leadership race (Harrison 2002).

The candidate who defeated Day in the 2002 leadership race, Stephen Harper, was much more successful. Under Harper, the party moderated its image and committed itself to securing power. Under Harper's leadership the Canadian Alliance merged with the PCs (now led by Peter McKay) to form the Conservative Party of Canada (CPC) in 2004. This united Conservative Party formed a minority government in January 2006 and won a renewed minority mandate in the fall of 2008. These organizational developments paralleled a move to a moderate and tightly disciplined style of politics.[1] Even during Harper's leadership and the return to a brokerage style of politics, the Conservative Party of Canada has maintained a place for social conservatives. Harper does not have particularly close ties to social conservatives, but they have enjoyed more prominence in the party under his leadership than under any previous Conservative leader (with the exception of Day). As the debate over same-sex marriage in 2005 showed, social conservatism has defined important parts of the party's public image. By doing away with the old Progressive Conservative norm that kept social issues out of politics and Reform's populist norm that rendered their place ambiguous at a time when social conservatism seemingly offered electoral opportunities, these changes allowed social conservatives to establish their political legitimacy. This legitimacy allowed them to continue as an important part of the party even after the departure of their preferred leader, the influx of other, 'Progressive' Conservatives, and the commitment of the new party to winning office through brokerage politics.

Canadian social conservatives have also moderated their tactics and language since the CPC won office in 2006. Social conservatives have continued to be seen as legitimate by others in the party, but their positions are less central to the party's overall appeals than they were during the debates over same-sex marriage. This is not surprising – social conservatives were defeated on a core issue and did not attract the voters to the party they had hoped to, but the very reasons for their decline point to their achievement of 'normal' status. No longer is their role minimized because they are seen to be illegitimate. Rather, their prominence within the party, like that of any other group, is dependent on their ability to achieve political success. Moreover, they seem to have accepted this situation themselves. Those who have not felt comfortable with this new role have changed their focus and now try to work more in local civil society than through partisan politics.

Social Conservatives and the Canadian Alliance

The Canadian Alliance was the result of Preston Manning's effort to unite the Canadian right and set it on a broader footing. With Clark's federal PCs uninterested in joining with the Canadian Alliance, the latter party formalized ties between Reformers and PCs from the more conservative Alberta and Ontario provincial parties. The process created considerable resistance from die-hard populists among Reformers, but their resistance was overcome by Manning's still significant command of party organization and resources (Ellis 2005). Manning had no significant difficulty in creating a new party, but he faced a serious challenge to his leadership from Stockwell Day.[2] Day, Alberta's treasurer at the time, proved more adept than Manning at signing up new members – a key advantage given the one-member, one-vote rule of the leadership race. To some extent, this was the result of Day's promise to be a youthful, telegenic, and bilingual politician who would be able to reach out to the vote-rich east. Day also benefited from disillusionment with the party's repeated failures to become the government and the support of a significant number of Reform MPs and Alberta MLAs (a point stressed in Harrison 2002).

Another part of Day's ability to attract new members was his recruitment of evangelical Christians and pro-life activists. Day worked hard to build up support in these communities and often used the language of social conservatism and evangelical Christianity to appeal to them.[3] As a result, Day was able to convince many that he was a more 'Christian' candidate than Manning and would be less inclined to the kind of compromises that Manning's populism had made, in the eyes of many social conservatives, on gay rights and abortion. In the last weeks of the leadership campaign, Manning did try to counter the efforts of Day's team to portray him as an un-Christian candidate by being more open about his own faith commitments. This effort proved to be too little, too late. Given Manning's long-established position that religious beliefs were best kept separate from political positions, it seems that there is little he could have done that would have satisfied this group entirely. For Day and his supporters, as their statements on same-sex marriage (among other issues) show, there was a specifically Christian approach to politics and a truly Christian politician would act in a definitely Christian way.

The optimism that surrounded Day at the time of his leadership evaporated quickly. He was initially seen by many as a media-savvy leader who would finally achieve the party's long-awaited electoral breakthrough in Ontario (Harrison 2002). During the 2000 election campaign, though, he was disorganized and prone to gaffes (Ellis 2001, 2005). After the election, Day proceeded to alienate many of the party's senior staff and a significant portion of its parliamentary caucus. These problems exploded on 15 May 2001 when eight MPs resigned from the party. By July, the number of dissidents had grown to thirteen, including senior party members Deborah Grey and Chuck Strahl. This group of dissidents formed their own Democratic Reform Caucus (DRC). Over the summer, this group entered into negotiations with the PC party and, in the fall, co-operated with them in the House. Eventually, this pressure caused Day to announce definite plans to resign the leadership, though with the caveat that he would run to succeed himself as leader of the party. In a formal leadership race that ran from December 2001 to March 2002, Stephen Harper defeated Day. Harper did not, however, purge any of Day's supporters from the party. Day himself received an important shadow cabinet position and many of his supporters continued to play important roles in the party. Many of the social conservatives that Day had mobilized also stayed in the party.

Stephen Harper had more experience in federal politics than Day. He had risen to prominence with a speech at the first Reform convention and had become an important policy adviser in the party's early development. Becoming a Reform MP in 1993, he was soon the most prominent public figure in the party after Manning himself. Harper's youth and talent led many to believe that he was also a possible successor to Manning. Tension between Harper and Manning, and perhaps simple impatience, led Harper to resign from the party in 1997 to join the National Citizens' Coalition, a conservative think tank. While never far from politics, he was an inactive partisan until 2001, when he returned to politics to contest the Canadian Alliance leadership (Johnson 2005).

On social and religious issues, Harper has kept his personal views relatively quiet. He seems, though, to lean towards a laissez-faire stance on such issues. While personally opposed to the extension of gay rights to include marriage, he had argued that Reform should take no position at all on gay rights or moral matters and, as early as the mid-1990s, favoured the creation of civil unions that would recognize same-sex couples (Johnson 2005). On abortion, he has said only that his views are 'in-between' and that he would not introduce legislation on the topic (CBC 2004). Social conservatives saw Harper in his early years as rather ambivalent about their goals. Many inside the party believed his closest advisers – such as old Reformers like Tom Flanagan, or Mulroney Tories like Hugh Segal and Marjorie Le Breton – were cool to social conservatives at best and hostile to them at worst. Some (MacDonald 2010, Martin 2010) have implied that Harper has become closer to and more influenced by social conservatives in the last few years, but the evidence we have about the internal workings of the party since it formed government suggests that this is not the case.

Whatever Harper's personal beliefs about social conservatism, they have been subsumed into his broader goal of refashioning the party into an efficient electoral machine. To this end, he has worked hard to minimize strife between different factions in the party and to craft party platforms that have wide appeal in the electorate. This pattern became apparent with his successful incorporation of Day's supporters and the dissident Democratic Reform Caucus into the rest of the Canadian Alliance after his leadership victory. He followed this exercise with negotiations with Peter MacKay (who had replaced Joe Clark as PC leader in 2003) to unite the two parties.[4] Negotiations between the two party leaders led to a memorandum of understanding in October 2003 about the terms on which the two parties could be merged. This was followed by Harper's victory in the contest to lead the new, united party in March 2004. Harper's successful creation of the Conservative Party of Canada (CPC) out of the Progressive Conservative and Canadian Alliance parties was followed by what most observers saw as a reasonably successful 2004 election campaign. The Liberals were reduced to a minority government and the Conservatives had positioned themselves on the centre-right as the government in waiting (Ellis and Woolstencroft 2004). In the 2006 and 2008 campaigns, Harper followed an even more moderate brokerage strategy and successfully won a minority government (Plamondon 2006, Ellis and Woolstencroft 2006). His governments have been characterized by tightly disciplined backbenchers and Cabinet, as well as frequent brinkmanship between the Conservatives and the other parties, usually in situations where none of the players stand to gain from an election. While clearly on the right, the Harper government has been far more moderate than would have been expected if one had predicted the path taken by a Harper government based on his earlier views.

Despite this moderate strategy and his defeat of Day in the leadership race, Harper did not try to drive social conservatives out of the party after his victory and has proved somewhat responsive to their concerns. Indeed, as both party leader and prime minister, Harper has departed from the previous practice of brokerage politicians in Canada by positioning the party on the socially conservative side of the same-sex marriage debate. While he continued the old Progressive Conservative and Reform practice of allowing free votes on contentious moral issues, he has also not been afraid to identify the party as wholly in opposition to the extension of gay rights.

Same-Sex Marriage

These transformations in party politics were going on at the same time as court challenges to the existing heterosexual definition of marriage were making social issues central to Canadian politics. Attempts to change the definition of marriage through legal action had been going on for some time. The first verdict on these cases was delivered in October 2001, when a British Columbia judge upheld the existing common-law (heterosexual) definition of marriage. Decisions at the trial level in Ontario (*Halpern*) and Quebec (*Hendricks*) the following summer decided that the exclusion of same-sex couples from civil marriage was discriminatory. In both cases, the court gave the government two years to pass a law extending the right to marry to same-sex couples. Should Parliament not pass such a law in that time, same-sex marriage would become permissible under Canadian law on the basis of these decisions. The couples concerned appealed these rulings, arguing that the two-year waiting period for the decisions to take effect was unjust. In May 2003, the BC Court of Appeals agreed with the Quebec and Ontario rulings – same-sex marriages should be recognized and gave the legislature two years to change the laws (Rayside 2008).

Hearings before the Ontario Court of Appeal were heavily contested, with the federal government calling as witnesses socially conservative academics like Daniel Cere and Katherine Young (see Cere and Farrow 2004, Young and Nathanson 2004). The federal argument was that same-sex unions could not be called marriage because of the traditional linkage of marriage and procreation. This argument, and the suspended implementation of the earlier decisions, was overturned in June 2003 when the Ontario Court of Appeal ordered the City of Toronto to issue marriage licences to same-sex couples immediately. It was followed by similar decisions in the BC Court of Appeal in July 2003 and the Quebec Court of Appeals in March 2004.

While there was some discussion at the Cabinet level about whether the Chrétien government would appeal the Ontario court's decision, the government decided that it would not. Instead, it referred three questions to the Supreme Court of Canada:

1. Is the definition of marriage within the exclusive legislative authority of the government of Canada?
2. Is same-sex marriage consistent with the Canadian Charter of Rights and Freedoms?
3. Does the Freedom of Religion guaranteed by the Charter protect religious officials from being compelled to perform a marriage between two persons of the same sex that is contrary to their religious beliefs? (Larocque 2006, 154)

The Supreme Court hearings on these reference questions began on 6 October 2004. In its response to the reference, the Supreme Court ruled that the definition of marriage was within federal jurisdiction, that same-sex marriage was completely consistent with the Charter, and that religious officials were protected by the freedom of religion clause in the Charter should they choose not to perform a same-sex marriage. The court refused to answer the fourth question (whether an opposite-sex only definition of marriage was constitutional) that the new Martin government had attached, arguing that same-sex marriage had largely already been recognized by judicial decisions and the federal government's own decision not to appeal lower-court decisions to the Supreme Court. What remained to be determined after the string of court decisions was whether the government would simply allow them to stand, introduce a bill to conform Canadian legislation with the court rulings, or – as some conservatives were calling for – use the Charter's notwithstanding clause to maintain the traditional opposite-sex definition of marriage.

This series of court cases was paralleled by very significant social movement activity on both sides of the debate. Pro-same-sex-marriage groups like EGALE, Canadians for Equal Marriage, the United Church, various labour unions, and many human rights groups presented briefs and organized grass-roots activity. Opponents also organized. The organizations examined in previous chapters (REAL Women, the Canadian Council of Catholic Bishops, the Evangelical Fellowship of Canada, Focus on the Family Canada, and Campaign Life) continued to play central roles. They were joined by several ad hoc groups formed specifically to organize against same-sex marriage and by Focus on the Family Canada. Of these new groups, only the umbrella organization Defend Marriage Canada was more than an organizational letterhead for a single activist (such prominent one-man shows included Equipping Christians for the Public Square, Concerned Christians Canada, and 4 My Canada) (Malloy 2009). All of these organizations built on concerns that had been growing on the right about the definition of marriage throughout the 1990s and early 2000s.

Debates in Parliament over changing the definition of marriage took place with this social movement and judicial activity in the background and as the Canadian partisan right was sorting out its organizational form. In Parliament, both the Bloc and the NDP imposed party discipline to support the extension of gay rights from the mid-1990s forward, making them clearly the parties of social progressivism. The Liberals were divided. Indeed, until the Ontario, BC, and Quebec court rulings extended the right to marry to same-sex couples, the Chrétien government had been fairly active in opposing the extension of marriage rights to same-sex couples. After the Ontario court decision, Chrétien and his cabinet reversed course and prepared a draft bill extending the definition of marriage in tandem with their Supreme Court reference.

From about 2000 on, the Progressive Conservatives also took part in debates over the extension of gay rights. Their major and representative intervention was in 2003, when the Liberal government introduced Bill C-23, the Modernization of Benefits Act. The bill, which passed, extended to same-sex couples the equivalent government benefits enjoyed by opposite-sex couples. Though not yet leader, Peter MacKay was the party's major voice in the debate. He argued that the bill was about fairness and equality, not about morality or marriage, and protested that the furore over the bill was distracting attention from more important issues. At the same time, he was careful to state that, for him 'personally,' marriage was between a man and a woman (MacKay 15 February 2000).

Debate over the bill began during the transformation of the Reform Party into the Canadian Alliance. Eric Lowther was, as he had been throughout the 1990s, in the forefront of opposition to the bill. And, as before, Lowther and Canadian Alliance MPs like him offered a mix of populist and socially conservative arguments against the bill.[5] Compared with the language of previous debates, however, there was far less emphasis on populist themes and more on socially conservative ones. Grant McNally argued that 'the guiding philosophy of our day and our society, I would propose, is something called personal subjective relativism.' For him, issues like the extension of gay rights were not so much religious as philosophical: either one believes truth can be absolute and so opposes the bill, or believes all things are relative and subjective and so supports it. He spoke of how in 1968 the 'government started its assault on tradition, family, and marriage' (McNally 3 April 2000). Jim Pankiw was even explicitly partisan, arguing that 'we are a pro-family party as opposed to the anti-family policies of the federal government' (Pankiw 3 April 2000).[6]

MPs were also more likely to offer explicitly religious arguments than they had been during previous debates. Jim Hart 'spoke out on behalf of a minority group in the country, that group being Christians . . . I speak out on behalf of the traditions, society, and foundations we have here in Canada' (21 February 2000). He went on to argue that 'the union of a man and a woman is something sacred in this country' (21 February 2000), but that the government was not doing enough to promote and protect family life. Paul Forseth, another CA MP, quoted from Corinthians to express his opposition to same-sex marriage (3 April 2000) while Garry Breitkreuz quoted from the Gospels (3 April 2000). The statements of Canadian Alliance MPs mark a major change, for a significant number explicitly took substantive social conservative positions, frequently grounded them in religious teaching, and identified their party with those positions.

After this debate, and after Day's leadership ended, the question of where social conservatives fit in the Conservative Party of Canada became an issue in the 2004 election. This had not been the CPC plan, as they (and the other opposition parties) had been successful early in the campaign at keeping debate focused on the sponsorship scandal that was afflicting the government. In a series of ads, though, the Liberals countered that Harper's Conservatives had a hidden agenda to transform Canada into something like George W. Bush's United States. The damage done by these ads was exacerbated late in the campaign when Conservative MP Randy White said that he thought laws prohibiting discrimination against homosexuals should be repealed and that a Conservative government would use the notwithstanding clause to repeal a same-sex marriage bill. When combined with earlier comments by Cheryl Gallant comparing abortion to the beheading of hostages by terrorists and an ill-advised press release asking whether Paul Martin approved of child pornography, the Conservatives had a difficult time resisting the charge that they were a party committed to social conservatism (Johnson 2005, Ellis and Woolstencroft 2004).

Despite these problems, the Conservatives did reasonably well in the election, winning 30 per cent of the popular vote and ninety-nine seats. As the other opposition parties had also done well, the Liberals formed a minority government. While all parties expected only a short time before the next election, it was enough of a space for the Conservatives to improve the organization of their party and sort out policy. Central to this project was the work to formulate a definitive policy platform for the party and to solidify its hurriedly constructed organization. This process culminated in a policy convention 17–19 March 2005 in Montreal.[7] Built on discussion groups that had gone on at the local level for some time, the convention was tightly scripted. It had the goals of reaching out to Quebec voters, making the party appear moderate, and using the publicity from the convention as a springboard to a successful election campaign (Plamondon 2006).

Bill C-38 (the Civil Marriage Act) had already been introduced into the House at the time of the convention, and, while the convention maintained substantively the same platform on same-sex marriage on which the party had fought the election, social conservatives made gains by having definite commitments to their positions made part of the party platform:

i) The Conservative Party believes that the family unit is essential to the well-being of individuals and society, because that is where children learn values and develop a sense of responsibility . . .
ii) The Conservative Party believes that Parliament, through a free vote, and not the courts should determine the definition of marriage. A Conservative Government would support the freedom of religious organizations to determine their own practices with respect to marriage.
iii) The Conservative Government will support legislation defining marriage as the union of one man and one woman. (CPC 2005, 22)

Social conservatives' efforts from the convention floor to get a plank on abortion placed on the platform were soundly rebuffed. One leading social conservative, former PC MP Elsie Wayne, was booed off the stage after a speech in which she referred to abortion as 'baby-killing.' The convention settled on platform statement that 'a conservative government will not support any legislation to regulate abortion' (CPC 2005, 20). The party has maintained this stance on domestic issues to the present day.

Debates over same-sex marriage began again when C-38 was introduced in Parliament on 1 February 2005. Debate over the bill lasted late into June and overlapped not only with the Conservative policy convention but also with a very unstable political situation. The Liberals narrowly survived a confidence motion in early May and were able to pass a budget only after Conservative Belinda Stronach defected and independent Chuck Cadman agreed to support the government. Martin's whipping of his Cabinet to support C-38 was controversial: two ministers resigned from Cabinet, two MPs left the party, and thirty-two Liberal backbenchers voted against the bill. Even with the support of the NDP (which imposed party discipline on the vote), most of the BQ caucus, and a handful of Conservatives, it was not clear until late in June that the bill would actually pass, such was the opposition of the Liberal backbenches to the bill.

Despite the heated political atmosphere, the CPC allowed a free vote on C-38. Aside from the three MPs who voted for the bill, the party was remarkably unified, with ninety-three of its MPs voting against it. Conservative MPs voting against the government motion generally agreed that they would like to see a compromise enacted along the lines that Harper laid out in his response to the introduction of the bill. He argued that 'marriage is a fundamental distinct institution, but that same-sex couples can have equivalent rights and benefits and should be recognized and protected' (16 February 2005). In the rest of his speech, he argued that such a compromise was legally defensible without using the section 33 override clause and was in keeping with the preferences of most Canadians. He also tried to make clear that, for him personally, the issue was not a religious one but, rather, the protection of a traditional institution from state interference. He also expressed concern that the bill would threaten religious freedom.

Aside from those who voted with the Liberals, Conservative MPs generally followed the lines laid down by the policy convention and Harper's speech. All MPs argued that civil unions would be preferable to extending the definition of marriage to include same-sex couples. They argued that such a solution would extend all of the legal rights of marriage to same-sex couples, but would retain the traditional recognition that opposite-sex marriage was a unique institution. There was also general agreement that, on such an important issue, Parliament, in a free vote, had both the right and the responsibility to speak for the popular will against court decisions. Some added that progressive European countries had reached compromise positions on same-sex marriage, others that the United Nations Human Rights Tribunal had argued that the traditional definition of marriage could be retained without infringing on the rights of gays and lesbians. Most also took the more partisan line that the Liberals were being inconsistent, as Martin and many of his senior colleagues had voted for the Reform motion defining marriage in traditional terms in 1999.[8]

While often drawing on these themes, and never disagreeing with them, more socially conservative MPs added other arguments. They especially stressed the point that the traditional family, with two parents, did a better job of raising children than other family models. This, social conservatives argued, reinforced the notion that procreation was a central part of the definition of the family and of marriage. They also argued that allowing same-sex marriage represented a harmful shift from a child-centred model of family to an adult-centred one.[9] A number of social conservatives explicitly grounded their arguments in personal faith commitments. Several quoted religious leaders or texts as the basis for their decisions, some going so far as to quote scripture into Hansard. Others preferred to describe how their beliefs prevented them from supporting the extension of the definition of marriage. Some argued that changing the definition of marriage showed how far into relativism society was falling.[10]

Despite the passage of C-38, in the summer of 2005 conservative activists still hoped that a Conservative government would work to repeal the bill. In response, Harper made it one of his 2006 campaign promises that a Conservative government would introduce and allow a completely free vote on a motion to repeal the Civil Marriage Act. In December 2006, he kept this promise by introducing a motion asking the House to call on the government 'to introduce legislation to restore the traditional definition of marriage without affecting civil unions and while respecting existing same-sex marriages' (7 December 2006). This unusual legislative step – in essence the government was asking the House for permission to introduce legislation – saw only brief debate before being defeated 175 to 123. In the debate, Conservative MPs spent far more time arguing that there was a need for continued debate than they did debating for a substantive position one way or the other. Harper had made it clear before debate on the motion that he would only return to the issue once, so that the defeat of the motion effectively ended his concern with same-sex marriage.

Since the end of the debate over same-sex marriage, issues of central concern to social conservatives have not been as prominent as they were during the first half of the decade. This, compounded by the great difficulty in gaining access to central players since the CPC formed the government, makes it hard to completely assess the place that social conservatives currently have in the party. There are a number of indications, though, that suggest they have retained their legitimacy within the party but, given their lack of success at attracting new voters or winning policy battles, are not as prominent as they were in the early 2000s.

One indication of this combination of legitimacy and little influence is that there have been only three items on the legislative agenda that can be seen as socially conservative initiatives as of 2011. Two are relatively minor, have been presented in a low-key fashion, and have not attracted a great deal of media attention. The first was an increase in the age of consent for sexual activity. This measure had been introduced several times in one form or another after the Conservatives formed government but only passed at the end of March 2008 as part of an omnibus criminal justice bill. Somewhat more controversial have been repeated efforts to introduce, through private member's bills, 'unborn victims of crime' legislation. Leon Benoit introduced such a proposal in May 2006. It made it as far as committee before stalling in the face of objections that it was unconstitutional. Some argue that this was due to the bill's poor drafting, others that the constitutional argument was merely a cover for the government to remove a controversial measure from the legislative agenda (Reid 2008). In revised form, introduced by Ken Epp in the fall of 2007, this bill came before the House in the spring of 2008 as Bill C-484. While in public this measure has been described as a minor and commonsensical change to Canadian law, social conservatives see it as an important incremental move toward restricting abortion (Reid 2008).

One issue that generated substantial debate was the international maternal health initiative that the government introduced in the spring of 2010 and was to be a key part of Canada's policy platform as it hosted the G8 and G20 summits that summer. When introduced by Foreign Minister Lawrence Cannon and International Co-operation

Minister Bev Oda, the $1.1 billion initiative would have refused funding for contraception and abortion. Two days after the announcement, Harper retreated from this position when he allowed contraceptives to be funded, but did not move on the abortion aspect of the bill, stating that 'we do not want a debate, here or elsewhere, on abortion' (CBC News 18 March 2010). The government maintained this position in the face of criticism from the United States and the United Kingdom and a fierce debate domestically, the highlight of which was a motion from the Quebec National Assembly that unanimously supported freedom of choice. This suggests that this is not the beginning of a powerful wave of social conservatism: the government has made clear that it will not support in any way the introduction of private member's bills concerned with abortion. Precisely why the Harper government has taken the stance on foreign aid that it has is unclear, but it cannot be seen as part of a wider campaign against the Canadian status quo on abortion.

This more low-key approach has a been a part of what both social conservatives close to the party and party insiders who are definitely not social conservatives (Le Breton 2006) have described as an effort by social conservatives who remained engaged in politics to become better.[11] No longer do social conservative elites in the party feel it appropriate to articulate their views at any cost, nor do they see the articulation of principles as their primary purpose in politics. Instead, the vision they pursue is one that seeks incremental change in their favour, but only when the pursuit of that change does not endanger the party's chances of staying in office. They have come to believe that they ought to focus their attention primarily on goals they have a chance of achieving.

To be sure, a good part of this change in attitude must be attributed to the defeat of social conservatives in debates over same-sex marriage. On such symbolic issues, however, defeat does not always mean the end of activism – the American social conservative movement has been remarkably resilient in the face of policy setbacks. Rather, the situation of the party and a change in attitudes among the social conservative elite seem to be at the root of the change. What these changing attitudes marks is the recognition of social conservatives as being a part of 'normal politics.' They are able to argue for some of their convictions as long as their arguments do not endanger the place of the party as a whole.

While the evidence for this change is, admittedly, only impressionistic, it also seems that there has been a shift in the attitudes of grass-roots social conservatives (Reid 2008, Clemenger 2008). Many of these grass-roots activists, disappointed by the outcome of the same-sex marriage debates, have withdrawn somewhat from politics. They still hold the same views, but have begun to emphasize action at the local level through voluntary and church-based organizations. On abortion, for example, there has been a shift in interest away from lobbying parties and government to operating community-based organizations such as Birthright. Others, while unhappy that they did not win on same-sex marriage, have decided that it is still worth being involved in politics in the hope of gaining incremental advances (Reid 2008).

In short, the period since 2005 has seen a moderation of social conservative demands as some activists exit partisan politics and others become more like traditional brokerage politicians. This has not been because they have been forced out of the party. Rather, they have shifted to a more 'normal' model of political involvement. Social conservatives are still allowed a seat at the conservative table but must prove they can contribute to the party's success – proof they have been unable to supply.

Conclusion

The debate over same-sex marriage shows the extent to which norms around social issues changed in Canada between 1968 and 2007 and how those changing standards have affected the political mobilization of social conservatives. In 1968, Canadian conservatives were careful not to take specifically religious positions on social issues or to link a position on a social issue to other political issues. Throughout the 1980s, during heated public debates over abortion, the PCs continued to keep social issues isolated from other topics as matters of personal conscience. Initially, the Reform Party's populist ideology and powerful leadership prevented that party from taking a socially conservative position on abortion, leading to an outcome on that issue very similar to that of the Progressive Conservatives. With the decentralization of the party and the emergence of same-sex marriage as the major social issue (Ellis 2005), Reform took on a definitively social conservative colouring.

This change was cemented during the United Alternative process. Since the selection of Stockwell Day as Canadian Alliance party leader in 2000, social conservatives have emerged as a part of the conservative coalition in Canada. This was due not only to their ability to mobilize, but also to a more general acceptance by other conservatives that their concerns and positions were politically legitimate. This shift gave social conservatives the ability to mobilize within right-wing Canadian parties. It led to their continued presence and – at some important junctures – prominence. While they are certainly not dominant, they have been more prominent since Day's emergence, despite his defeat by Stephen Harper, and the Conservative Party of Canada's trend towards moderation since then.

What these changes represent is the disappearance of norms, held by both populists and conservatives, that placed social issues outside of partisan politics. Canadian conservatives now see social issues as 'normal' political issues to be decided by the party as a whole, given the electoral ramifications of any particular position. That this norm held for so long after social issues had become a part of the political debate is an important factor – along with Canada's less favourable political culture and more centralized party institutions – in making Canadian social conservatives less powerful than their American counterparts.

Conclusion

The characterization of social conservatism presented here rests on two interrelated arguments. The first concerns the nature of social conservatism: that it represents one response to the political challenges posed by changing social mores but that it is not the only possible conservative response to the politicization of the personal. As chapter 1 explored, how conservatives responded to this challenge was rooted in how they understood the boundaries between politics and social life and, to a lesser but still significant extent, in their view of the appropriate relationship between religious belief and political action.

This first argument suggests a fundamental similarity between social conservatives in Canada and the United States. To paint the picture solely in terms of ideological similarity, however, is to ignore the very real practical differences between social conservatism in Canada and the United States that the second, historical-comparative, argument highlights. In the United States, most conservative efforts between the Second World War and the 1970s went into the creation of a social movement. Within this movement, traditionalists were relatively rare and had more affection for religion than did their Canadian counterparts. Similarly, many American laissez-faire conservatives saw the United States as a nation that was both virtuous and free – giving substantial traction to concerns about the decline of public virtue. Social conservatives were able to draw on existing themes to build alliances with other conservatives. These alliances meant that conservatives of all sorts worked together to gain control of the Republican Party during the late 1970s. Their success in this enterprise, and the recognition that social conservatives should have as prominent a place in the party as in the movement, came with Reagan's 1980 election victory.

Since 1980, social conservatives have been able to retain their place within the Republican Party through both good and bad times. On key issues like same-sex marriage and abortion, they have ensured that the party always positions itself on their side of these divisive issues. Other American conservatives have been generally happy to recognize the claims of social conservatives, but they are not willing to forgo their own priorities for the sake of the social conservative agenda. When social conservatives overreached – most notably, 1988–92 – controversy over policy and the control of party offices resulted. The controversies during these periods, though, were not over whether social conservatives had a place in the party but what, precisely, that place was. Events since 2008 – for example, John McCain's selection of Sarah Palin as a running mate and some themes in the Tea Party movement – suggest that we should expect social conservatism to maintain a prominent place in the Republican Party.

In Canada, the natural hesitancy of those conservatives who draw on classical liberalism to have the state regulate social mores was reinforced by a strong group of traditionalists who saw taking a political stance on social issues as un-conservative, for political action on such questions brought inappropriate questions of religion and personal morality into politics. Such conservatives, by and large, were not keen on extending access to abortion or allowing equal rights for gays and lesbians, they were even less eager to trigger political turmoil on such topics. It was better, they believed, to frame these issues as ones of personal morality on which a political party had no business taking a particular position. During controversies over abortion during the 1960s, 1970s, and 1980s the Progressive Conservative Party of Canada held itself to this position. The Reform Party's declaration that abortion was a topic of private morality best dealt with by plebiscite or other mechanisms of direct democracy illustrates that that party, initially, held to a similar position.

It was only when the major issue under contention shifted from abortion to gay rights, and after a period of electoral failure and institutional turmoil within the Reform Party, that social conservatives were able to brand Reform as sympathetic to their cause and to win space on its platform. They solidified their position during Stockwell Day's leadership of the Canadian Alliance. Day's tenure as leader was short-lived, but it confirmed the recognition by other conservatives that social conservatives were legitimate political partners for other conservatives. Once part of the mainstream of the Canadian Alliance and the Conservative

Party of Canada, social conservatives continued to deal with the challenges imposed by a political system that stresses strong party discipline and a political culture not terribly sympathetic to their concerns.

This mainstreaming of social conservatism in the party was the result of an implicit bargain – social conservatives would receive recognition and policy influence only if they sought minor changes that did not jeopardize the party's standing in the polls. For their part, the social conservatives who remain active in party politics after their defeat on the question of same-sex marriage agreed to prioritize the party's electoral success over efforts to advance their own agenda. Those unhappy with this deal seem to have redirected their efforts back into social movements and the creation of third-sector organizations. While this seemed to promise incremental progress for social conservatives in Canada during the mid-2000s, the bargain may now seem to have tied those who remain active in party politics into a system over which they have little influence and – given Canadian political culture and tight party discipline – little chance of building the sort of momentum that their American counterparts continue to enjoy.

The limitations that these environmental factors pose for social conservatives in Canada have been very clear since the end of the debate over same-sex marriage in 2005. Revisiting the debate over same-sex marriage has been off the table for the party since its motion to reignite the debate failed in the House of Commons. A murmuring of debate around abortion during the spring of 2010 produced a more complicated outcome, the political origins of which are currently unclear but the outcomes of which point to the limits of growth for social conservatism in Canada. The re-emergence of debate over abortion was triggered by the Conservative government's introduction of a funding initiative to improve maternal health in the Third World as part of a coordinated international effort on the topic. Uniquely – and in the face of criticism from the American and British governments and from the Liberals, NDP, and Bloc – the Canadian government's approach to the problem denied funding for abortions as part of the package. Had developments ended there, it might have seemed that social conservatives had managed to get the Harper government to enact something analogous to the Hyde Amendment in the United States. Perhaps to dispel such a reading of the situation, the prime minister then made a point of stating that he would impose party discipline to ensure that Conservative MPs voted against any private member's bill that would restrict access to abortion. To be sure, such a bill would have no chance of passing the

Canadian Parliament, but Harper's clear positioning of the party is a dramatic change. If, in the late 1990s, Canadian conservatives accepted the politicization of the personal and took an ideologically motivated approach to the questions, the discussions around abortion during 2010 suggest that the party may be in the midst of another shift – one that accepts that the personal is political, but sees it as the terrain for brokerage politics rather than ideological stands. Given the broader context of Canadian politics, there is little reason to believe that such a return to brokerage politics will do anything to further social conservatism in Canada.

Knowing that social conservatism's place in the political firmament is a result of similar processes of evolution, but very different starting points in different environments, in Canada and the United States, allows us to make certain projections about its future. To the extent that social conservatives are defined by an opposition to the changes in sexual mores associated with the 1960s, their hopes of long-term success are greatly limited by the absence of any evidence that traditional beliefs about family structure or sexual life are gaining ground in the population. Instead, most evidence indicates that the substantive beliefs that have motivated social conservatives are in decline among the general population. Public attitudes toward abortion are reasonably stable and same-sex relationships are increasingly socially acceptable in the two countries (though Americans are slightly more conservative than Canadians on both issues). Premaritial sex and cohabition are generally accepted. Issues like stem-cell research and euthanasia, which social conservatives see as closely linked to abortion and the 'culture of death,' have not mobilized new allies for social conservatives.

Absent a major change in social dynamics, this analysis suggests the decline of social conservatism. Social conservatives' rise to prominence in the face of adverse social trends and policy defeats has been predicated on gaining respectability and visibility within party organizations and then using those organizations to promote their agenda. This they have achieved in Canada and the United States, but their limited ability to change public policy shows the limits of their influence in the bureaucracy and, often, the judiciary. Furthermore, despite their best efforts, they have been unable to influence society in a way that might make their views more generally pervasive, and so more attractive to office-seeking parties. As the societal base on which they have built their activism declines and the shock factor of their emergence wears off, organizational successes will be unable to offset such global decline. At the same time, having become full members of the conservative coalition means that social conservatives will maintain their close ties to conservative parties and, as a result, continue to give those parties a socially conservative quality. This trend will be more marked in the United States than in Canada, given their already greater strength and the larger part of the population to whom they can appeal.

An expectation that social conservatism will become more muted should not, however, be understood as a sign of the declining importance of religion in politics. While it is true that we have witnessed a decline in religious observance in general, Canada and the United States have frequently experienced the ebb and flow of religious involvement in politics. Perhaps the fading of social conservatism should create expectations for a change in the places where faith and politics rub up against each other, just as social conservatism itself obscured the emphasis on social justice and civil rights that marked religious interventions in politics during the 1960s. Certainly, the difficulty that some parts of both societies have integrating Muslims points to a future where questions of religious diversity are more pressing than they have been for the last generation. Similarly, a set of court cases in Canada around religious liberty (for example, the right of justices of the peace not to marry same-sex couples and of fundamentalist Mormons to practise polygamy) suggest ongoing debates on that topic as well.

If the eventual fading of social conservatism should not be understood as representing the end of religion as a point of contention in our politics, nor should it be seen as representing an end to conservatism as a potent force in politics. To be sure, social conservatives have made an important contribution to both the ideological character and electoral success of conservatives parties in Canada and the United States. This book has focused on them as the conservative group that, for the past two generations, has most strongly challenged mainstream culture while posing central questions about the appropriate nature of our politics. They have not at any time, however, been the dominant group. The concerns that have been most often acted upon are those of laissez-faire conservatives – especially their desire to reduce government's involvement in the economy. This part of conservatism shows no sign of abating and seems to be continuing its increasing dominance not just of the right's economic policies, but of mainstream fiscal policy in general. By offering particular versions of this vision, laissez-faire conservatives will be able to continue successfully appealing to voters.

Notes

Introduction

1 The reading of social conservatism presented here is closer in its analysis to the characterization of evangelical influence presented by Jonathan Malloy in his 2009 article and a number of conference papers.

2 Key comparative examples of this style of work are Panebianco (1988), Kirchheimer (1966), von Beyme (1985), Duverger (1954), Ostrogorski (1902), Michels (1915), and Epstein (1967). On American parties, Epstein (1967), Aldrich (1995), and Wattenberg (1991) are landmarks. Similarly important Canadian studies of party organization include Carty (2002), Carty, Cross, and Young (2000), Brodie and Jenson (2007), Perlin (1980), Wearing (1981), and Whitaker (1979).

3 For overviews of this approach see Peters (1999); Steinmo (2001); Rhodes, Binder, and Rockman (2006); Thelen (1999); as well as Hall and Taylor (1996). March and Olsen (1984, 1989) set the theoretical underpinnings for the new institutionalism. Berman (1998) applies it to the study of political parties.

4 Choosing to emphasize the institutional setting of social conservative activism brings in its train a particular set of methodological requirements which move the study from description through the analysis of the norms held by political elites. The descriptive aspect of this book is, in one sense, methodologically straightforward. It entails identifying moments when social conservatives attempted to influence party politics, describing the debates and interactions that occur around these episodes, and placing them in a sequence. While collecting data on some of these episodes is difficult – for how are we to know what really went on behind the scenes? – this task can be accomplished through a fairly standard political historian's

combination of archival research, interviews, and examination of relevant published materials. By carefully comparing the narratives presented by interviewees with that constructed out of archival material and the work of scholars and journalists we can go a long way towards describing and understanding specific phenomena in discrete historical circumstances. Care must be taken to balance the biases inherent in the viewpoints of different sources, and no single source can ever be completely relied upon, but wherever the situation can be examined through overlapping sources (preferably of different types) there can be reasonable confidence in the resulting account. The chronicling aspect of the study is methodologically uncontroversial but, in practice, quite difficult. And it should be acknowledged in advance that gathering information from these sources was not as completely successful as might have been hoped. In Canada, archival material was relatively plentiful, published material (especially Hansard) gave a representative selection of the views of major players, and a wide selection of actors were generous with their time and gave interviews. In the United States, by contrast, the relevant archival materials were widely scattered, as were the speeches and accounts of key players. Further, interviews with those inside the party were difficult to come by (though movement activists did offer many insights). This situation is unfortunate, though it has been partially rectified through the use of the very extensive secondary literature on social conservatism in the United States. As a result, the Canadian chapters offer a novel empirical investigation while the American chapters are in keeping with standard scholarly opinion on the topic.

5 Rayside (2008, 19–60) offers a full and useful account of these differences as they have impacted mobilization for the recognition of sexual diversity.

1. Conservative Ideology and Social Change

1 Other thinkers who typify traditionalism in the last part of the twentieth century include Michael Oakeshott, Russell Kirk, and – though only in some aspects of his thought – George Grant.

2 Hayek's economic thinking was influential, too, but pride of place on the economic side should go to his fellow Nobel Prize laureate Milton Friedman. For Friedman's political statements see his *Capitalism and Freedom* (1962).

3 Though it also included a chapter on 'Radical Feminism.'

4 Gairdner thinks that religion is important to society but denies that Christianity plays any direct influence on his thinking. In his personal life, he describes himself as a non-observant Christian (Gairdner 2005).

5 While social conservatives have tried to use their positions on marriage, gay rights, abortion, and education to build bridges to Muslims, Hindus, and Jews, it is only with the latter group, and only with a small minority within it, that they have met with any degree of success.

6 The statement and a number of useful essays on the reasons for and barriers to political cooperation between Evangelical Protestants and Catholics are contained in Colson and Neuhaus (1995). Neuhaus was a prolific author and, as editor of the journal *First Things,* active in both the practical and intellectual sides of political questions and a leading figure in Protestant-Catholic-Jewish ecumenical efforts. Much of *Catholic Matters* (Neuhaus 2006) is an autobiographical account of his activities. Linker (2006) provides a critical but insightful account by a former associate. See Neuhaus (1997) for his description of his place in the inter-conservative debates of the mid-1990s.

2. American Conservatism before Ronald Reagan

1 Rae (1989) and Reinhard (1983) are the best examinations of the place of liberals and conservatives in the Republican Party during this period.

2 On Goldwater, see his autobiography *With No Apologies* (1979), as well as Goldberg's (1995) and Edwards's (1995) biographies. Perlstein (2001) and Middendorf (2006) offer two different views of the importance of the campaign. Middendorf's is particularly interesting, for he was the campaign's treasurer. For a contemporary and critical view by a journalist see White (1965).

3 While language like this illustrates the openness of American conservatism to religious views, it is true that Goldwater's fundamental commitment was to individual freedom. Most famously, by the 1980s he was openly pro-choice on abortion and of the opinion that 'every good Christian ought to kick Falwell right in the ass. I get so damned tired of these political preachers telling me what to believe and do' (cited in Goldberg 1995, 315).

4 It is not possible to over-emphasize that 'social problems' had and continue to have a double meaning in the United States that they lack in Canada. In both the United States and Canada, social issues include issues like the definition of marriage, gay rights, and abortion. In the United States, however, the deeply divisive civil rights struggle of the 1960s underpinned many of these issues with questions of race. Activism on other issues often carries echoes of the struggle over civil rights. See Carmines and Stimson (1989) for an examination of this phenomenon. Phillips (1969) and Scammon and Wattenberg (1970) are two treatments of this change that were very influential for Republicans in the 1970s.

5 On Nixon, a good, short introduction is Morgan (2002). Mason (2004) provides an excellent overview of his relationship with the Republican Party. The definitive Nixon biography is Ambrose's three-volume work (1987, 1989, 1991). On the place of conservatives in his (and Ford's) administration, see Reichley (1981). Nixon's own memoirs (1978) are extensive, though they are clearly exercises in rehabilitating his reputation.

6 The official biography of Reagan before 1980 (Morris 1999) is less than satisfactory. More useful are the two detailed biographies by Cannon (1982, 2000). Hayward (2001) is a useful study of the political environment of the day.

7 The year 1976 was also the last time a Republican platform would include support for the ERA: a conservative plank to rescind the traditional plank in support of the amendment did not make it out of committee. Conservatives did, though, manage to pass a platform plank calling for the 'enactment of a constitutional amendment to restore protection of the right to life for unborn children' (quoted in Critchlow 2007, 150).

8 The literature on this first generation of neoconservatives is large and of generally high quality. For overviews of the movement see Blumenthal (1986), DeMuth and Kristol (1995), Friedman (2005), Frum (1994), Gerson (1996), and Kristol (1995).

9 There has been little scholarly work done on the reaction of the fusionist movement to racial questions. Probably the strongest analysis is that of Carter (1995, 1996).

10 The literature on abortion politics in the United States is vast, but for useful histories of the first twenty years of the debate see Saletan (2003), Blanchard (1994), and Craig and O'Brien (1993). Adams (1997) is the best study of the parties' initial response in Congress. Tatalovich (1997) is a useful overview of the situation in Canada and the United States. Interviews with Donald Devine (2006), Richard Land (2006), and Gary Jarmine (2006) were also very helpful.

11 In terms of the groups involved and the language used, this state-level debate paralleled the debate over the abortion provisions of the Omnibus Bill in Canada in 1968.

12 In contrast to Canada, the American Catholic hierarchy took a strong stance against abortion quite early. See Byrnes (1991) on the American response and Cuneo (1989) on the Canadian reaction.

13 Opposition to abortion was to prove sufficiently strong to overcome long-standing confessional divides between activists. While Baptists and Catholics might have different views on alcohol, for example, activists from both traditions were united in their opposition to abortion. They soon

discovered the benefits of working together on other issues like pornography or gay rights (Devine 2006, Land 2006, Jarmine 2006).

14　William F. Buckley Jr's brother James, a Conservative Party senator from
New York, was an important figure in this early attempt to amend the
constitution. Another Buckley relation, brother-in-law Brent Bozell II, un-
dertook the first militant pro-life demonstration when he and the Sons of
Thunder, an ultra-right Catholic organization, occupied a Washington, DC,
abortion clinic in May 1970 (*Time* magazine, 29 March 1971).

15　Brown points out that the leaders of both Stop-ERA and Women Who
Want to Be Women were included in Paul Weyrich's coalition-building
efforts in the late 1970s. Rymph (2005) and Critchlow (2005) are useful
sources on how feminist and social conservative forces competed with
each other within the Republican Party during this time. Mansbridge
(1987) is an insightful and fair-minded history of the debate over
the ERA.

16　On this transition in evangelical attitudes see Bruce (1988), Martin (1996),
Oldfield (1996), Wilcox and Larson (2006), and Wald and Calhoun-Brown
(2007).

3. Ronald Reagan, George H.W. Bush, and Social Conservatism

1　Interviews conducted during 2006 with Gary Jarmine (then of Christian
Voice), Richard Land (of the Southern Baptist Convention), and J. Donald
Devine (then a Republican Party activist) confirmed these details. Each of
them had been active at a high level in the social conservative movement
during the late 1970s.

2　Roman Catholics made up a substantial part of the conservative movement's leadership and were one of the groups that Republicans hoped to
attract by appealing to their sense of social order. As voters and activists,
however, they did not move in large numbers towards the Republicans
and the Religious Right organizations until the late 1990s (Appleby 1997).

3　Pat Buchanan's 1992 campaign was as much populist as socially conservative and did not garner significant support.

4　See also Guth (1996) and Wilcox (2000) on this point.

5　On the American pro-life movement during the 1980s, see McKeegan
(1992); see also the essays by pro-life leaders in Wagner (2003). Doan (2007)
and Solinger (1998) are useful overviews.

6　For different views of Reagan's relationship with social conservatives
during his presidency see Crawford (1980), Edwards (1999), Frum (1994),
Schneider (2003), Ranney (1981), as well as the biography by Cannon (2000).

7 The administration's delay in responding to the epidemic can likely be attributed to social conservative activism.

8 See Oldfield (1996), Martin (1996), Moen (1992), and Wilcox (1992) for the
campaign; see Clifton (2004) and Wilcox (2006) for its long-term effects on
the Republican Party.

9 Aside from the question of gays serving in the military that emerged
during the 1992 campaign, the Bush presidency seems not to have been
much engaged in questions of gay and lesbian rights, even as the issue
was becoming increasingly important to social conservatives and was
percolating at lower levels of the judiciary and government. See Rimmerman (1996, 2002).

4. Social Conservatism and the Republican
Party from 1993 to the Present

1 On the Christian Coalition see Moen (1992), Oldfield (1996), Martin (1996),
and Wilcox and Larson (2006).

2 On Newt Gingrich and the Republican revolution see Gingrich (1995), Rae
(1998), Ashford (1998), Rae and Campbell (1999), McSweeney and Owens
(1998). Gingrich was forced to resign as Speaker of the House in 1998 following allegations of both financial and personal misconduct.

3 Although unsuccessful in the presidential race, the Republicans did maintain a majority, albeit a diminished one, in the House and gained two seats
in the Senate.

4 As Guth (1996) illustrates, this was a lesson that many social conservatives
at the state level were still learning during the late 1990s.

5 See Rimmerman (2002) for an overview.

6 In South Carolina Bush benefited most from the support of Religious Right
leaders as, with their support, he was able to paint McCain as soft on abortion. This was despite McCain's strong pro-life record (Crotty 2001, Wilcox
2002).

7 The extent to which this mobilization helped the Republicans is a matter
of some debate in the academic literature. See Green, Rozell, and Wilcox
(2003), Campbell (2007), and McMahone, Rankin, Beachler, and White
(2005) for different perspectives.

5. The Progressive Conservatives and the Boundaries of Politics

1 See also Horowitz (1966), Grant (1965), and MacQuarrie (1965, 1992).

2 Perlin (1980) stresses the affective, rather than ideological, roots of these
internal divisions, but, for our purposes, his insights and those of Christian

and Campbell point in the same direction – that the Progressive Conservatives were prone to factionalization.

3 It is striking that Canada's pre-eminent conservative intellectual during this period, George Grant, came to very different conclusions, particularly regarding abortion. For him, legalized abortion handed liberalism a 'cup of poison' (1998, 72) that 'weaken[ed] the very idea of rights itself' (1986, 119) and put us 'well on the road . . . to the horrors of the death camp and the purge' (1986, 119). However, as with other aspects of his thought, his arguments seem to have been ignored by those active in party politics.

4 Epp (2005) and Redway (2006).

5 See Tatalovich (1997) for an overview of Canadian opinion on abortion. For overviews of the Canadian abortion debate see Brodie (1992), Campbell and Pal (1991), Collins (1985), and Morton (1992). Cuneo (1989) is an insightful sociological study. Tatalovich (1997) gives a useful comparative perspective.

6 One of the bill's mechanisms may have also limited Catholic opposition. It allowed hospitals to set up therapeutic abortion committees (made up of doctors) to oversee the procedures. In many instances, this structure more or less allowed abortion on demand. But Catholic hospitals, by refusing to create such committees, could prevent the pre-conditions for legal abortions from being present on their premises.

7 Hereafter, citations in this form are to speeches in the House of Commons.

8 On the rarity of and reasons for free votes in the Canadian House of Commons see Flanagan (1997).

9 I would like to thank an anonymous activist who was heavily engaged in the movement during this period for granting me an interview. The point, with reference to the Roman Catholic part of the pro-life movement, is well substantiated by Cuneo (1989).

10 NDP MP Bill Blaikie did break with his party's otherwise uniformly pro-choice position.

11 Personal interview in 2006 with an anonymous caucus member.

12 Epp (2005), Stackhouse (2005), Le Breton (2006), and Edwards (2005).

13 Crosbie (2006), Edwards (2005), MacDonald (2005), and Epp (2005).

6. Social Conservatives and the Reform Party of Canada

1 As befits a third party, scholars have given Reform's ideology (Laycock 2002) and the beliefs of its members (Archer and Ellis 1994, Ellis 2005) substantial attention. Nevertheless, scholars have not reached any consensus on the place of social conservatism in the ideological mix that the Reform

Party articulated. One school of thought, exemplified by Laycock (1994, 2002), treats the Reform Party as a party of the New Right. In this view, the party seamlessly combined populism with a right-wing espousal of small government and limited politics. It offered a vision of society that stressed the role that the market can play in dealing with material needs and that the family can play in providing a social safety net and education. This was a widespread reaction to the pressures of societal change, shared by parties in continental Europe (Laycock 2002), Thatcher's Tories in Great Britain, and American conservatives (Harrison 1995). In this view, the party's position on social issues like abortion or gay rights derives from the foundational New Right notion that the state must be limited. In addition, such scholars see the New Right's generalized preference for undifferentiated individual rights rather than differentiated minority rights as an articulation of social conservatism (Laycock 2002). The other view, exemplified by Foster (2000) and Patten (1996, 1999), argues that the party was 'fraught with tensions' because of the difficulties in reconciling competing populist and conservative tendencies within it (Patten 1999, 29). Foster (2000) points out that the populism inherent in the party's formation often diffused or limited social conservatives' activism in the party. For those on the New Right, according to Foster, coming to a consensus on economic or constitutional issues was far easier than finding a unified position on social issues. This sense of a tension in the party over social issues is shared by Harrison, who notes that 'potential internal conflict extend[s] to other moral issues, in particular the abortion question' (Harrison 1995, 213). As the account that follows makes clear, the evidence I have found makes the second account the more credible one.

2 Though there were some prominent early disputes over immigration, most notably the party's opposition to the wearing of turbans by Sikh RCMP officers.

3 At the same time, it is fairly easy to expand this language to include these two core social conservative claims. See, for an example, Gairdiner (1990, 1992).

4 Later in the 1990s, euthanasia was added to the specific category of moral decisions. In the 1996 *Democratic Populism II* Report it was suggested that this category of 'moral issues' was too vague to be satisfactory analytically and this vagueness leads to 'policy gridlock . . . as party members assert various issues to be moral ones, and thus not subject to legitimate debate by party members' (9). Instead, it was suggested that the section be recast as a 'Referendums and Citizens Initiative' section of the *Blue Book* that would have issues concerning Canada's 'basic social fabric' (immigration,

language, and measurement) and issues of 'personal conscience' (abortion and capital punishment) as necessitating direct popular action (Reform Party 1996, 10). This suggested change, which was shelved as the United Alternative process began, amplifies the point made by the original wording – there were a variety of issues that the party marked off as outside the legitimate boundary of politics.

5 Indeed, it is probably safe to surmise that more of the party's membership saw it as an opportunity to oppose immigration and cultural change in Canada (Ellis 2005, Harrison 1995).

6 This speech was delivered to faculty and students of Regent College, a private Christian college. It is similar in content to a talk, also in the Manning archives at the University of Calgary, that he gave to the Missionary and Alliance Church of Calgary (his home congregation) on 1 June 1991. It should be taken, therefore, as a consistent part of his political thinking and, as addresses given to groups likely very amenable to the notion that religious beliefs ought to play a direct role in politics, as an honest portrayal of his own beliefs.

7 Reform's position on abortion remained relatively consistent: a party whose grass roots and leadership was predominantly pro-life consistently argued that the issue should be resolved in a referendum. Issues which social conservatives link to abortion, most notably euthanasia, emerged during the 1990s but never grew to the point that they became flashpoints for partisan contention (Ellis 2005).

8 Clemenger (2005), Epp-Buckingham (2005), and Gentles (2005).

9 Clemenger (2005), Epp-Buckingham (2005), and Gentles (2005).

10 MPs who made such positions the major part of their argument included Diane Ablonczy, Leo Benoit, Ken Epp, Jim Gouk, Elwin Hermanson, Ian McClelland, Robert Mills, Michael Scott, and Darrell Stinson.

11 Manning notes that neither Ringma nor Chatters were part of the family caucus. That is, they were not among the self-identified social conservatives in the party who saw issues of family and gender as especially important. Rather, they were both Reformers who had gotten involved in politics for other reasons (Manning 2002).

12 Liberal member Tom Wappel did introduce a private member's bill in April 1998 to define marriage as a union between persons of the opposite sex. However, it was not deemed votable, so that it only received an hour of debate in the House and then was dropped from the order paper (Wappel 9 October 1998). See Harrison (2002), Manning (2002), Ellis (2005), and Segal (2006) for different accounts of this attempt to unite the Canadian right.

7. Social Conservatives and the Unified Canadian Right

1 Johnson's biography of Stephen Harper (2005) argues that under his leadership the party moved back towards a moderate Canadian version of conservatism. Segal (2006) makes the same argument, but seeks to show that the new Conservative Party follows in the tradition of the old Progressive Conservatives. Plamondon (2006) offers an overview of the process of unifying the PC and Canadian Alliance parties down to the 2005 election. Unfortunately, a lack of access to key figures renders MacKey's (2005) examination of the place of religion in the party and in Stephen Harper's own thinking less than complete. Ellis (2001) stresses how the United Alternative process and the Canadian Alliance marked a return to brokerage politics by Canadian conservatives. Woolstencroft (2000) emphasizes the problems of the PC Party before the merger and how the party had little choice but to merge with the Canadian Alliance. Ellis and Woolstencroft (2004, 2006) portray today's Conservative Party of Canada (CPC) as following in the brokerage tradition of other large Canadian parties.
2 Ontario Tory strategist Tom Long was the only other significant contender for leadership of the new party.
3 One self-described libertarian party insider suggested that this difference could be partly attributed to a difference in evangelical theology. Many evangelicals, like Manning, were hesitant to be politically involved at all, let alone openly mix faith and politics. Alternatively, other Canadian evangelicals, like Day, saw themselves as a minority who needed to come out of the closet (a phrase frequently heard in evangelical circles) to articulate their own unique approach to politics. See Stiller (2003) for a discussion of this point and Harrison (2002) for examples of the types of appeals that Day made to social conservatives.
4 As leader, MacKay worked to define the party in traditionally Progressive Conservative terms, seeking a moderate position that made a fairly clear divide between the personal espousal of traditional morality and the necessary political goal of extending respect and equality to all (Plamondon 2006).
5 See also Chuck Strahl (3 April), Diane Ablonczy (3 April), Monte Solberg (3 April), Ken Epp (3 April), Jim Reynolds (3 April), Gerry Ritz (10 April), John Williams (10 April), Rick Casson (10 April), Myron Thompson (10 April), and Randy White (10 April).
6 Other MPs speaking in this vein included Robert Mills (3 April), Maurice Vellacott (3 April), and Lee Morrison (3 April).
7 The author was able to attend this convention as a student-observer.

8 MPs taking this line in their speeches in the House of Commons included Moore, Skellon, Williams, O'Connor, Forseth, Smith, Kamarnicki, Allison, Toews, Hiebert, Mills, Merrifield, Kamp, Gurmant Grewal, Nina Grewall, Casson, Finley, Fitzpatrick, Miller, Epp, Fletcher, Watson, Mark, Batters, Cummins, Hinton, Schellenberger, Warawa, Nicholson, Tweed, Yelich, Poillievre, Bezan, Tilson, Johnston, MacKay, Harrison, Ambrose, Benoit, Preston, Menzies, Reid, Guergis, Anderson, Anders, Goodyear, Benoit, Brown, Hinton, Harris, and Lukiwski.

9 In speeches in the House, these MPs included O'Connor, Pallister, Vellacott, Hill, Ablonczy, Scheer, Merrifield, Schmidt, Breitkreuz, Thompson, Komarnicki, Jean.

10 These included Warawa, Werner Schmidt, Duncan, Goldring, David Anderson, Day, Dale Johnston, Lunney, Hanger, Yelich, Doyle, Solberg, Prentice, Penson, Breitkreuz, Ritz, Myron Thompson, and Scheer.

11 Reid (2008), Hughes (2006), Clemenger (2008), and Le Breton (2006).

Bibliography

A Note on Interviews and Hansard

A number of people took the time to have conversations with me but have preferred to remain anonymous. I thank them very much for their time, as well as those who spoke on the record. In addition to those who granted interviews, I owe a thank-you to Ian Brodie for allowing me access to the 2005 Conservative policy convention as a student-observer, and to the organizers of the 2006 March for Life and 2006 Conservative Political Action Conference in Washington, DC. Prior to 1993, all *Commons Debates* are taken from the printed version. After 1993, all *Commons Debates* are from the stable electronic version for the relevant day.

Adams, Greg. 1997. Abortion: Evidence of Issue Evolution. *American Journal of Political Science*, 41(3): 718–37.

Adams, Michael. 2003. *Fire and Ice: The United States, Canada, and the Myth of Converging Values.* Toronto: Penguin.

Aldrich, John. 1995. *Why Parties? The Origin and Transformation of Party Politics in America.* Chicago: University of Chicago Press.

Ambrose, Stephen. 1987. *Nixon*, vol. 1: *The Education of a Politician, 1913–1962.* New York: Simon and Schuster.

– 1989. *Nixon*, vol. 2: *The Triumph of a Politician, 1962–72.* New York: Simon and Schuster.

– 1991. *Nixon*, vol. 3: *Ruin and Recovery, 1973–1990.* New York: Simon and Schuster.

The Anti-Abortion Campaign. 1971. *Time*, 29 March, n.p.

Appleby, R. Scott. 1997. Catholics and the Christian Right: An Uneasy Alliance. In *Sojourners in the Wilderness: The Christian Right in Comparative*

Perspective, ed. Corwin E. Smidt and James M. Penning, 93–115. Lanham, MD: Rowman and Littlefield.

Archer, Keith, and Faron Ellis. 1994. Opinion Structure among Party Activists: The Reform Party of Canada. *Canadian Journal of Political Science,* 27(2): 277–308.

Ashbee, Edward. 2007. *The Bush Administration, Sex, and the Moral Agenda.* Manchester: Manchester University Press.

Ashford, 1998. The Republican's Policy Agenda and the Conservative Movement. In *The Republican Takeover of Congress,* ed. Dean McSweeney and John Owens, 96–117. London: Macmillan.

Berman, Sheri. 1998. *The Social Democratic Moment: Ideas and Politics in the Making of Interwar Europe.* Cambridge: Harvard University Press.

Beyme, Klaus von. 1985. *Political Parties in Western Democracies.* Aldershot: Gower.

Biette, David. 2006. Personal interview with author. 11 January. Washington, DC.

Black, Amy, Douglas Koopman, and David Ryden. 2004. *Of Little Faith: The Politics of George W. Bush's Faith-Based Initiatives.* Washington, DC: Georgetown University Press.

Blanchard, Dallas A. 1994. *The Abortion Movement and the Rise of the Religious Right: From Polite to Fiery Protest.* New York: Twayne.

Blumenthal, Sidney. 1986. *The Rise of the Counter-Establishment: From Conservative Ideology to Political Power.* New York: Time Books.

Brennan, Mary C. 1995. *Turning Right in the Sixties: The Conservative Capture of the GOP.* Chapel Hill: University of North Carolina Press.

Breitkreuz, Garry. 7 May 1996. Speech to the House of Commons. http://www2.parl.gc.ca/housechamberbusiness/ChamberHome.aspx.

– 3 April 2000. Speech to the House of Commons. http://www2.parl.gc.ca/housechamberbusiness/ChamberHome.aspx.

Brodie, Janine. 1992. Choice and No Choice in the House. In *The Politics of Abortion,* ed. Janine Brodie, Jane Jenson, and Shelley Gavigan, 57–117. Toronto: Oxford University Press.

Brodie, Janine, and Jane Jenson. 2007. Piercing the Smokescreen: Stability and Change in Brokerage Politics. In *Canadian Parties in Transition,* 3rd ed., ed. Alain-G.Gagnon and A. Brian Tanguay, 33–55. Peterborough: Broadview.

Brown, Judie. 2 February 2006. Email to author.

Brown, Ruth Murray. 2002. *For a Christian America: A History of the Religious Right.* Amherst: Prometheus.

Bruce, Steve. 1988. *The Rise and Fall of the New Christian Right: Conservative Protestant Politics in America, 1978–1988.* Oxford: Clarendon Press.

Buckley, William F. 1964. Notes Towards and Empirical Definition of Conservatism. In *What Is Conservatism?* ed. Frank S. Meyer, 210–26. New York: Holt, Rinehart, and Winston.

Busch, Andrew E. 2005. *Reagan's Victory: The Presidential Election of 1980 and the Rise of the Right.* Lawrence: University of Kansas Press.

Bush, George W. 1999. *A Charge to Keep.* New York: William Morrow.

Byfield, Link. 2005. Personal interview with author. 23 August. Edmonton, AB.

Byrnes, Timothy A. 1991. *Catholic Bishops in American Politics.* Princeton: Princeton University Press.

Cameron, Mark. 2005. Personal interview with author. 22 June. Ottawa, ON.

Campbell, David E. 2007. The 2004 Election: A Matter of Faith. In *A Matter of Faith: Religion in the 2004 Presidential Elections,* ed. David E. Campbell, 1–15. Washington: Brookings.

Campbell, David E., and J. Quin Monson. The Case of Bush's Reelection: Did Gay Marriage Do It? In *A Matter of Faith: Religion in the 2004 Presidential Elections,* ed. David E. Campbell, 120–42. Washington: Brookings.

Campbell, Kim. 1996. *Time and Change: The Political Memoirs of Canada's First Woman Prime Minister.* Toronto: Doubleday.

Campbell, Robert M., and Leslie A. Pal. 1991. *The Real World of Canadian Politics,* 2nd ed. Peterborough, ON: Broadview.

Canadian Broadcasting Corporation (CBC). 2004. No Plans to Change Abortion Law: Harper. 1 June 2004. http://www.cbc.ca/news/canada/story/2004/06/01/harpabort040601.html.

Cannon, Lou. 1982. *Reagan.* New York: G.P. Putnam.

– 2000. *President Reagan: The Role of a Lifetime.* New York: Public Affairs.

Carlson-Thies, Stanley. 2006. Personal interview with author. 16 February. Washington, DC.

Carmines, Edward, and James Stimson. 1989. *Issue Evolution: Race and the Transformation of American Politics.* Princeton: Princeton University Press.

Carter, Dan. 1995. *The Politics of Rage: George Wallace, the Origins of the New Conservatism, and the Transformation of American Politics.* New York: Simon and Schuster.

– 1996. *From George Wallace to Newt Gingrich: Race in the Conservative Counterevolution, 1963–1994.* Baton Rouge: Louisiana State University Press.

Carty, R. Kenneth. 2002. The Politics of Tecumseh Corners: Canadian Political Parties as Franchise Organizations. *Canadian Journal of Political Science,* 35 (4): 723–45.

Carty, R. Kenneth, William Cross, and Lisa Young. 2000. *Rebuilding Canadian Party Politics.* Vancouver: UBC Press.

Ceasar, James, and Andrew Busch. 1993. *Upside Down and Inside Out: The 1992 Elections and American Politics*. Lanham, MD: Rowman and Littlefield.

– 1997. *Losing to Win: The 1996 Elections and American Politics*. Lanham, MD: Rowman and Littlefield.

Cere, Daniel, and Douglas Farrow, eds. 2004. *Divorcing Marriage: Unveiling the Dangers in Canada's New Social Experiment*. Montreal and Kingston: McGill-Queen's University Press.

Chipeur, Gerald. 2005. Personal interview with author. 20 August. Calgary, AB.

Christian, William, and Colin Campbell. 1974. *Political Parties in Canada*. Toronto: McGraw-Hill Ryerson.

– 1996. *Party Politics and Ideologies in Canada*, 3rd ed. Toronto: McGraw-Hill Ryerson.

Cigler, Allan J., Mark Josyln, and Burdett A. Loomis. 2003. The Kansas Christian Right and the Evolution of Republican Politics. In *The Christian Right in American Politics: Marching to the Millennium*, ed. John C. Green, Mark J. Rozell, and Clyde Wilcox, 145–67. Washington: Georgetown University Press.

Clarke, Harold, Jane Jenson, Lawrence Leduc, and Jon Pammett. 1984. *Absent Mandate: The Politics of Discontent in Canada*. Toronto: Gage.

Clemenger, Bruce. 2005. Personal interview with author. 23 June. Ottawa, ON.

– 2008. Telephone interview with author. 21 February.

Clifton, Brett. 2004. Romancing the GOP: Assessing the Strategies Used by the Christian Coalition to Influence the Republican Party. *Party Politics*, 10(5): 475–98.

Collins, Anne. 1985. *The Big Evasion: Abortion, the Issue That Won't Go Away*. Toronto: Lester and Orpen Dennys.

Colson, Charles, and Richard John Neuhaus, eds. 1995. *Evangelicals and Catholics Together: Toward a Common Mission*. Dallas, TX: Word.

Conger, Kimberly H., and John C. Green. 2002. Spreading Out and Digging In: Christian Conservatives and State Republican Parties. *Campaigns and Elections*, 23(1): 58–63.

Conley, Patricia. 2005. The Presidential Race of 2004: Strategy, Outcome, and Mandate. In *A Defining Moment: The Presidential Election of 2004*, ed. William Crotty, 108–36. Armonk, NY: M.E. Sharpe.

Conservative Party of Canada, 2005. *Policy Declaration*. http://www.conservative.ca/media/20050319-POLIC%20DECLARATION.pdf (accessed 18 May 2007).

Coulter, Ann. 1998. *High Crimes and Misdemeanors: The Case against Bill Clinton*. New York: Regnery.

Craig, Barbara Hinkson, and David M. O'Brien. 1993. *Abortion and American Politics.* Chatham: Chatham House Publishers.

Crawford, Alan. 1980. *Thunder on the Right: The 'New Right' and the Politics of Resentment.* New York: Pantheon.

Critchlow, Donald. 2005. *Phyllis Schlafly and Grassroots Conservatism: A Woman's Crusade.* Princeton: Princeton University Press.

– 2007. *The Conservative Ascendancy.* Cambridge: Harvard University Press.

Crosbie, John, with Geoffrey Stevens. 1997. *No Holds Barred: My Life in Politics.* Toronto: McClelland and Stewart.

Crosbie, John. 2006. Telephone interview with author. 18 August.

Crotty, William. 2001. The Presidential Primaries: Triumph of the Frontrunners. In *America's Choice 2000,* ed. William Crotty, 95–115. Boulder, CO: Westview.

Cuneo, Michael W. 1989. *Catholics against the Church: Anti-Abortion Protest in Toronto, 1969–1985.* Toronto: University of Toronto Press.

DeMuth, Christopher, and William Kristol, eds. 1995. *The Neo-Conservative Imagination: Essays in Honor of Irving Kristol.* Washington: AEI Press.

Dennis, Kim. 2006. Personal interview with author. 18 January. Washington, DC.

Devine, Donald J. 2006. Personal interview with author. 23 January. Washington, DC.

Diefenbaker, John G. 1969. Speech to the House of Commons, 27 January. *Commons Debates,* 28th Parliament, Session 1, volume V, 4834–9. Ottawa: Queen's Printer.

– 1969. Speech to the House of Commons, 18 April. *Commons Debates,* 28th Parliament, Session 1, volume VII, 7693. Ottawa: Queen's Printer.

– 1977. *One Canada.* Toronto: Macmillan.

Dinsdale, W.G. 1969. Speech to the House of Commons, 17 April. *Commons Debates,* 28th Parliament, Session 1, volume VII, 7639. Ottawa: Queen's Printer.

Doan, Alesha E. 2007. *Opposition and Intimidation: The Abortion Wars and Strategies of Political Harassment.* Ann Arbor: University of Michigan Press.

Durham, Martin. 2006. Evangelicals and the Politics of Red America. In *Right On? Political Change and Continuity in George W. Bush's America,* ed. Iwan Morgan and Philips Davies, 204–19. London: Institute for the Study of the Americas.

Duverger, Maurice. 1954. *Political Parties.* New York: Wiley.

Edwards, Jim. 2005. Telephone interview with author. 23 November.

Edwards, Lee. 1995. *Goldwater: The Man Who Made a Revolution.* Washington: Regnery.

– 1999. *The Conservative Revolution: The Revolution That Remade America.* New York: Free Press.

Ehrman, John. 1995. *The Rise of Neoconservatism: Intellectuals and Foreign Affairs 1945–1994.* New Haven, CT: Yale University Press.

Eldersveld, Samuel J., and Hanes Walton. 2000. *Political Parties in American Society,* 2nd ed. Boston: Bedford/St Martin's.

Ellis, Faron. 2001. The More Things Change . . . The Alliance Campaign. In *The Canadian General Election of 2000,* ed. Jon Pammett and Christopher Dornan, 59–91. Toronto: Dundurn.

– 2005. *The Limits of Participation: Members and Leaders in Canada's Reform Party.* Calgary: University of Calgary Press.

Ellis, Faron, and Peter Woolstencroft. 2004. New Conservatives, Old Realities. In *The Canadian General Election of 2004,* ed. Jon Pammett and Christopher Dornan, 66–106. Toronto: Dundurn.

– 2006. A Change of Government, Not a Change of Country: The Conservatives and the 2006 Election. In *The Canadian General Election of 2006,* ed. Jon Pammett and Christopher Dornan, 58–93. Toronto: Dundurn.

Epp, Jake. 2005. Personal interview with author. 20 July. Toronto.

Epp-Buckingham, Janet. 2005. Personal interview with author. 23 June. Ottawa, ON.

Epstein, Leon. 1967. *Political Parties in Western Democracies.* New York: Praeger.

Erwin, Lorna. 1993. Neo-Conservatism and the Canadian Pro-Family Movement. In *The Canadian Review of Sociology and Anthropology,* 30(3): 401–21.

Flamm, Michael W. 2005. *Law and Order: Street Crime, Civil Unrest, and the Crisis of Liberalism in the 1960s.* New York: Columbia University Press.

Flanagan, Tom. 1995. *Waiting for the Wave.* Toronto: Stoddart.

– 1997. The Staying Power of the Legislative Status Quo: Collective Choice in Canada's Parliament after *Morgentaler. Canadian Journal of Political Science,* 30(1): 31–54.

– 1998. *Game Theory and Canadian Politics.* Toronto: University of Toronto Press.

– 2001. From Reform to the Canadian Alliance. In *Party Politics in Canada,* 8th ed., ed. Hugh Thorburn, 280–92. Toronto: Pearson.

– 2005. Personal interview with author. 17 August. Calgary, AB.

– 2007. *Harper's Team.* McGill-Queen's University Press.

Forbes, Hugh Donald. 2007. *George Grant: A Guide to His Thought.* Toronto: University of Toronto Press.

Formicola, Jo Renee, Mary Segers, and Paul Weber. 2002. *Faith-Based Initiatives and the Bush Administration: The Good, the Bad, and the Ugly.* Lanham, MD: Rowman and Littlefield.

Forseth, Paul. 3 April 2000. Speech to the House of Commons. http://www2.
parl.gc.ca/housechamberbusiness/ChamberHome.aspx.

Foster, Bruce. 2000. New Right, Old Canada: An Analysis of the Political
Thought and Activities of Selected Contemporary Right Wing Organizations. PhD diss., University of British Columbia.

Freeden, Michael. 1996. *Ideologies and Political Theory: A Conceptual Approach.*
Oxford: Clarendon Press.

Friedman, Milton, and Rose Friedman. 1962. *Capitalism and Freedom.* Chicago:
University of Chicago Press.

Friedman, Murray. 2005. *The Neoconservative Revolution: Jewish Intellectuals and
the Shaping of Public Policy.* Cambridge: Cambridge University Press.

Frum, David. 1994. *Dead Right.* New York: Basic Books.

Gairdner, William. 1990. *The Trouble with Canada: A Citizen Speaks Out.* Toronto:
Stoddart.

– 1992. *The War against the Family: A Parent Speaks Out.* Toronto: Stoddart.

– 2005. Personal interview with author. 22 March. King City, ON.

Gentles, Ian. 2005. Personal interview with author. 25 April. Toronto.

Gerson, Michael. 1996. *Neoconservative Vision: From the Cold War to the Culture
Wars.* Lanham, MD: Madison Books.

Gilgoff, Dan. 2007. *The Jesus Machine: How James Dobson, Focus on the Family,
and Evangelical America Are Winning the Culture War.* New York: St Martin's
Press.

Gingrich, Newt. 1995. *To Renew America.* New York: Harper Collins.

Goertz, Dan. 2005. Personal interview with author. 31 March. Toronto.

Goldberg, Robert Alan. 1995. *Barry Goldwater.* New Haven: Yale University
Press.

Goldwater, Barry. 1964. *The Conscience of a Conservative.* Sheperdsville, KY:
Victor Publishing Co.

– 1979. *With No Apologies.* New York: Morrow.

Gottfried, Paul. 1993. *The Conservative Movement,* rev. ed. New York:
Twayne.

Grant, George. 1965. *Lament for a Nation.* Ottawa: Carleton University Press.

– 1986. *Technology and Justice.* Toronto: Anansi.

– 1998. *English-Speaking Justice.* Toronto: Anansi.

Grant, Robert. 2000. The Politics of Sex. In *The Politics of Sex and Other Essays,*
88–102. New York: Macmillan.

Green, John C., Mark Rozell, and Clyde Wilcox, eds. 2003. *The Christian Right
in American Politics: Marching to the Millennium.* Washington, DC: Georgetown University Press.

Greene, John Robert. 2000. *The Presidency of George Bush.* Lawrence: University Press of Kansas.

Grey, Deb. 2004. *Never Retreat, Never Explain, Never Aplogize: My Life, My Politics.* Toronto: Key Porter.

– 2006. Telephone interview with author. 10 November.

Guth, James L. 1996. The Politics of the Christian Right. In *Religion and the Culture Wars: Dispatches from the Front,* ed. John C. Green, James L. Guth, Corwin E. Smidt, and Lyman A. Kellstedt, 7–30. Lanham, MD: Rowman and Littlefield.

Hall, Peter A., and Rosemary C.R. Taylor. 1996. Political Science and the Three New Institutionalisms. *Political Studies,* 44: 936–57.

Harper, Stephen. 2005. Speech to the House of Commons, 16 February. http://www2.parl.gc.ca/housechamberbusiness/ChamberHome.aspx.

– 2006. Speech to the House of Commons, 7 December. http://www2.parl.gc.ca/housechamberbusiness/ChamberHome.aspx.

Harrison, Trevor. 1995. *Of Passionate Intensity: Right-Wing Populism and the Reform Party of Canada.* Toronto: University of Toronto Press.

– 2002. *Requiem for a Lightweight: Stockwell Day and Image Politics.* Montreal: Black Rose.

Hart, Jim. 2000. Speech to the House of Commons, 21 February. http://www2.parl.gc.ca/housechamberbusiness/ChamberHome.aspx.

Hayek, F.A. 1944. *The Road to Serfdom.* London: George Routledge and Sons.

– 1960. *The Constitution of Liberty.* Chicago: University of Chicago Press.

– 1964. Why I Am Not a Conservative. In *What Is Conservatism?* ed. Frank Meyer, 88–107. New York: Holt, Rinehart, and Wilson.

– 1973. *Law, Legislation and Liberty: Rules and Order.* Chicago: University of Chicago Press.

– 1976. *Law, Legislation, and Liberty: The Mirage of Social Justice.* Chicago: University of Chicago Press.

– 1979. *Law, Legislation and Liberty: The Political Order of a Free Society.* Chicago: University of Chicago Press.

Hayward, Steven F. 2001. *The Age of Reagan, 1964–1980: The Fall of the Old Liberal Order.* New York: Prima.

Herman, Didi. 1994. *Rights of Passage: Struggles for Gay and Lesbian Equality.* Toronto: University of Toronto Press.

Higgins, Michael, and Douglas Letson. 1990. *My Father's Business: A Biography of His Eminence G. Emmett Cardinal Carter.* Toronto: Macmillan.

Horowitz, Gad. 1966. Conservatism, Liberalism, and Socialism in Canada: An Interpretation. *Canadian Journal of Economics and Political Science,* 32(2): 141–71.

Hughes, Jim. 2006. Personal interview with author. 31 July. Toronto.

Hughes, Kent. 2006. Personal interview with author. 18 January. Washington, DC.

Hunt, Albert R. 1981. The Campaign and the Issues. In *The American Elections of 1980*, ed. Austin Ranney, 142–77. Washington, DC: American Enterprise Institute.

– 1985. The Campaign and the Issues. In *The American Elections of 1984*, ed. Austin Ranney, 129–46. Washington, DC: American Enterprise Institute.

Jarmine, Gary. 2006. Personal interview with author. 10 February. Washington, DC.

Jarvis, Mark. 2005. *Conservative Governments, Morality and Social Change in Affluent Britain, 1957–1964*. Manchester: Manchester University Press.

Jelen, Ted G. 2007. Life Issues: Abortion, Stem-Cell Research, and the Case of Terry Schiavo. In *Religion and the Bush Presidency*, ed. Mark J. Rozell and Gleaves Whitney, 197–213. New York: Palgrave Macmillan.

Johnson, William. 2005. *Stephen Harper and the Future of Canada*. Toronto: McClelland and Stewart.

Katz, Richard, and Robin Kolodny. 1994. Party Organization as an Empty Vessel: Parties in American Politics. In *How Parties Organize: Change and Adaptation in Party Organization in Western Democracies*, ed. Richard Katz and Peter Mair, 23–50. London: Sage.

Kirchheimer, Otto. 1966. The Transformation of Western European Party Systems. In *Political Parties and Political Development*, ed. J. LaPalombara and M. Wiener, 177–200. Princeton, NJ: Princeton University Press.

Kirk, Russell. 1953. *The Conservative Mind: From Burke to Santayana*. New York: Regnery.

Knopf, Rainer, and F.L. Morton. 2000. *The Charter Revolution and the Court Party*. Peterborough, ON: Broadview.

Koop, C. Everett. 1991. *Koop: The Memoirs of America's Family Doctor*. New York: Random House.

Koopman, Douglas C. 1996. *Hostile Takeover: The House Republican Party 1980–1995*. New York: Rowman and Littlefield.

Krasniunas, Nina Therese, and Jack E. Rossotti. 2007. President George W. Bush and Judicial Restraint: Accommodating Religion. In *Religion and the Bush Presidency*, ed. Mark J. Rozell and Gleaves Whitney, 235–55. London: Palgrave Macmillan.

Kristol, Irving. 1995. *Neo-Conservatism: The Autobiography of an Idea*. New York: Free Press.

Land, Richard. 2006. Telephone interview with author. 14 February.

Larocque, Sylvain. 2006. *Gay Marriage: The Story of a Canadian Social Revolution*. Trans. Robert Chodos, Louisa Blair, and Benjamin Waterhouse. Toronto: James Lorimer.

Laycock, David. 1994. Reforming Canadian Democracy? Institutions and Ideology in the Reform Party Project. *Canadian Journal of Political Science,* 27(2): 213–47.

– 2002. *The New Right and Democracy in Canada: Understanding Reform and the Canadian Alliance.* Don Mills, ON: Oxford University Press.

Layman, Geoffrey. 2001. *The Great Divide: Religious and Cultural Conflict in American Politics.* New York: Columbia University Press.

Le Breton, Marjorie. 2006. Telephone interview with author. 10 August.

Levant, Ezra. 2005. Personal interview with author. 17 August. Calgary, AB.

Link, William A. 2008. *Righteous Warrior: Jesse Helms and the Rise of Modern Conservatism.* New York: St Martin's Press.

Linker, Damon. 2006. *The Theocons: Secular America under Siege.* New York: Anchor.

Lowther, Eric. 1998. Speech to the House of Commons, 8 June. http://www2.parl.gc.ca/housechamberbusiness/ChamberHome.aspx.

– 1999. Speech to the House of Commons, 8 June. http://www2.parl.gc.ca/housechamberbusiness/ChamberHome.aspx.

MacDonald, Flora. 2005. Telephone interview with author. 10 November.

MacDonald, Marci. 2006. Stephen Harper and the Theo-Cons. *The Walrus,* October.

– 2010. *The Armageddon Factor: The Rise of Christian Nationalism in Canada.* Toronto: Random House.

MacKay, Peter. 2000. Speech to the House of Commons, 15 February. http://www2.parl.gc.ca/housechamberbusiness/ChamberHome.aspx.

MacKenzie, Chris. 2005. *Pro-Family Politics and Fringe Parties in Canada.* Vancouver: UBC Press.

MacKey, Lloyd. 2005. *The Pilgrammage of Stephen Harper.* Toronto: ECW Press.

MacQuarrie, Heath. 1965. *The Progressive Conservative Party.* Toronto: McClelland and Stewart.

– 1992. *Red Tory Blues.* Toronto: University of Toronto Press.

Malbin, Michael J. 1981. The Conventions, Platforms, and Issue Activists. In *The American Elections of 1980,* ed. Austin Ranney, 99–142. Washington, DC: American Enterprise Institute.

Malloy, Jonathan. 2007. A Temporary Surge? The State of Evangelical Activism after Same Sex Marriage. Paper presented at Gender, Religion, and Politics Conference, University of Toronto, 17–19 January.

– 2009. Bush/Harper? Canadian and American Evangelical Politics Compared. *Canadian Review of Canadian Studies,* 39(4): 352–63.

Manning, Preston. January 1988. Speech in Reform Party Archives.

– 1992. *New Canada*. Toronto: Macmillan.

– 2002. *Think Big: Adventures in Life and Democracy*. Toronto: McClelland and Stewart.

– 2005. Personal interview with author. 27 April. Toronto.

Mansbridge, Jane. 1987. *Why We Lost the ERA*. Chicago: University of Chicago Press.

March, James G., and Johan P. Olsen 1984. The New Institutionalism: Organizational Factors in Political Life. *The American Political Science Review,* 78(3): 734–49.

– 1989. *Rediscovering Institutions: The Organizational Basis of Politics*. New York: Free Press.

Marshall, Jennifer. 2006. Personal interview with author. 23 February. Washington, DC.

Martin, Lawrence. 2010. *Harperland: The Politics of Control*. Toronto: Viking.

Martin, William. 1996. *With God on Our Side: The Rise of the Religious Right in America*. New York: Broadway Books.

Mason, Robert. 2004. *Richard Nixon and the Quest for a New Majority*. Chapel Hill: University of North Carolina Press.

Mayer, William G. 2001. The Presidential Nominations. In *The Election of 2000,* ed. Gerald M. Pomper, 12–46. New York: Chatham House.

McClusky, Tom. 2006. Personal interview with author. 30 January. Washington, DC.

McKeegan, Michele. 1992. *Abortion Politics: Mutiny in the Ranks of the Right*. New York: Free Press.

McMahon, Kevin, David Rankin, and John White. 2005. *Winning the White House, 2004: Vote by Vote, Region by Region*. New York: Palgrave Macmillan.

McNally, Grant. 2000. Speech to the House of Commons, 3 April. http://www2.parl.gc.ca/housechamberbusiness/ChamberHome.aspx.

McSweeney, Dean, and John E. Owens, eds. 1998. *The Republican Takeover of Congress*. New York: St Martin's Press.

Ménard, Réal. 1995. Speech to the House of Commons, 26 April. http://www2.parl.gc.ca/housechamberbusiness/ChamberHome.aspx.

Meyer, Frank S. 1964a. Freedom, Tradition, Conservatism. In *What Is Conservatism?* ed. Frank S. Meyer, 1–17. New York: Holt, Rinehart, and Winston.

– 1964b. Consensus and Divergence. In *What Is Conservatism?* ed. Frank S. Meyer, 229–41. New York: Holt, Rinehart, and Winston.

Michels, Robert. 1915. *Political Parties: A Sociological Study of the Oligarchical Tendencies of Modern Democracy*. New York: Hearst.

Middendorf, John. 2006. *A Glorious Disaster: Barry Goldwater's Presidential Campaign and the Origins of the Conservative Movement*. New York: Basic Books.

Moen, Matthew. 1989. *The Christian Right and Congress*. Tuscaloosa: University of Alabama Press.

– 1992. *The Transformation of the Christian Right*. Tuscaloosa: University of Alabama Press.

Monson, J. Quin, and J. Baxter Oliphant. 2007. Microtargeting and the Instrumental Mobilization of Religious Conservatives. In *A Matter of Faith: Religion in the 2004 Presidential Election*, ed. David E. Campbell, 95–120. Washington: Brookings.

Morgan, Iwan. 2002. *Nixon*. London: Arnold.

Morris, Edmund. 1999. *Dutch: A Memoir of Ronald Reagan*. New York: Random House.

Morton, F.L. 1992. *Morgentaler v. Borowski: Abortion, the Charter, and the Courts*. Toronto: McClelland and Stewart.

Morton, F.L., and Rainer Knopff. 2000. *The Charter Revolution and the Court Party*. Peterborough, ON: Broadview.

Mulroney, Brian. 1988. Speech to the House of Commons, 28 November. *Commons Debates*, 38 Elizabeth II, volume 4, 6339–6343.

Murphy, Paul V. 2001. *The Rebuke of History: The Southern Agrarians and American Conservative Thought*. Chapel Hill: University of North Carolina Press.

Nash, George. 1976. *The Conservative Intellectual Movement in America since 1945*. New York: Basic Books.

Neuhaus, Richard John. 1984. *The Naked Public Square: Religion and Democracy in America*. Grand Rapids, MI: Eerdman's.

– 1997. The Anatomy of a Controversy. In *The End of Democracy? The Judicial Usurpation of Politics: The Celebrated First Things Debate with Arguments Pro and Con*. Dallas: Spence.

– 2006. *Catholic Matters: Confusion, Controversy, and the Splendor of Truth*. New York: Basic Books.

Nickerson, Dave. 1988. Speech to the House of Commons, 26 July. *Commons Debates*, 37th Parliament, Session 2, volume XIV, 18007–8. Ottawa: Queen's Printer.

Nixon, Richard. 1978. *The Memoirs of Richard Nixon*. New York: Grosset and Dunlop.

Nock, Albert J. 1943. *Memoirs of a Superfluous Man*. New York: Harper's.

Norquist, Grover. 2006. Personal interview with author. 3 February. Washington, DC.

Novak, Michael. 1982. *The Spirit of Democratic Capitalism*. New York: Simon and Schuster.

Olasky, Marvin. 2000. *Compassionate Conservatism*. New York: Free Press.

Oldfield, Duane. 1996. *The Right and the Righteous: The Christian Right Confronts the Republican Party*. Lanham, MD: Rowman and Littlefield.

Ostrogorski, Moisei. 1902. *Democracy and the Organization of Political Parties.* New York: Macmillan.

Panebianco, Angelo. 1988. *Political Parties: Organization and Power.* Cambridge: Cambridge University Press.

Pankiw, Jim. 1998. Speech to the House of Commons, 8 June. http://www2. parl.gc.ca/housechamberbusiness/ChamberHome.aspx.

– 2000. Speech to the House of Commons, 3 April. http://www2.parl.gc.ca/ housechamberbusiness/ChamberHome.aspx.

Patten, Steve. 1999. The Reform Party's Re-imagining of the Canadian Nation. *Journal of Canadian Studies*, 34(1): 27–51.

Peele, Gillian. 1984. *Revival and Reaction: The Right in Contemporary America.* Oxford: Clarendon.

– 1990. The Agenda of the New Right. In *The Reagan Presidency: An Incomplete Revolution,* ed. Dilys M. Hill, Raymond Moore, and Phil Williams, 29–48. London: Macmillan.

Peese, Ed. 2006. Personal interview with author. 9 February. Washington, DC.

Perlin, George. 1980. *The Tory Syndrome: Leadership Politics in the Progressive Conservative Party.* Montreal and Kingston: McGill-Queen's University Press.

Perlstein, Rick. 2001. *Before the Storm: Barry Goldwater and the Unmaking of the American Consensus.* New York: Hill and Wang.

Peters, B. Guy. 1999. *Institutional Theory in Political Science: The 'New Institutionalism.'* London and New York: Pinter.

Phillips, Kevin. 1969. *The Emerging Republican Majority.* New York: Arlington House.

Plamondon, Bob. 2006. *Full Circle: Death and Resurrection in Canadian Conservative Politics.* Toronto: Key Porter.

Plourde, Andre. 1988. Speech to the House of Commons, July 26th. *Commons Debates,* 37th Parliament, Session 2, volume XIV, 18019–21. Ottawa: Queen's Printer.

Pomper, Gerald M. 1985. The Nominations. In *The Election of 1984: Reports and Interpretations,* ed. Marlene Michels Pomper, 1–35. Chatham: Chatham House.

– 1993. The Presidential Election. In *The Election of 1992,* ed. Gerald M. Pomper, 132–57. New York: Chatham House.

Rae, Nicol C. 1989. *The Decline and Fall of the Liberal Republicans from 1952 to the Present.* New York and Oxford: Oxford University Press.

– 1998. *Conservative Reformers: The Republican Freshmen and the Lessons of the 104th Congress.* Armonk: M.E. Sharp.

Rae, Nicol C., and Colton C. Campbell. 1999. *New Majority or Old Minority? The Impact of Republicans on Congress.* New York: Rowman and Littlefield.

Ranney, Austin. 1981. *The Presidential Election of 1980.* Washington: AEI Press.

Rayside, David. 1998. *On the Fringe: Gays and Lesbians in Politics.* Ithaca, NY: Cornell University Press.

– 2008. *Queer Inclusions, Continental Divisions.* Toronto: University of Toronto Press.

Reagan, Ronald. 1984. *Abortion and the Conscience of the Nation.* New York: Thomas Nelson.

Redway, Allan. 2006. Personal interview with author. 26 July. Toronto.

Reform Party of Canada. 1990. *Blue Book.*

– 1993. Draft Statement on Homosexual Rights. 12 September. Series IX of Reform Party Fonds, University of Calgary Archives.

– 1994. Ottawa Assembly Proceedings. Series V of Reform Party Fonds, University of Calgary Archives.

– 1996a. Vancouver Assembly Proceedings. Series V of Reform Party Fonds, University of Calgary Archives.

– 1996b. *Democratic Populism II Report.* Series V of Reform Party Fonds, University of Calgary Archives.

Reichley, A. James. 1981. *Conservatives in an Age of Change: The Nixon and Ford Administrations.* Washington, DC: Brookings.

Reid, Aidan. 2005. Personal interview with author. 15 June. Ottawa, ON.

– 2008. Personal interview with author. 20 February. Ottawa, ON.

Reimer, Sam. 2003. *Evangelicals and the Contential Divide: The Conservative Protestant Subculture in Canada and the United States.* Montreal and Kingston: McGill-Queen's University Press.

Reinhard, David W. 1983. *The Republican Right since 1945.* Lexington: University Press of Kentucky.

Republican Party. 1976. Republican Party platform, as reported in the Congressional Record. http://www.ford.utexas.edu/LIBRARY/document/platform/platform.htm.

– 1980. Republican Party platform, as reported in the Congressional Record. http://www.presidency.ucsb.edu/showplatforms.php?platindex=R1980.

Rhodes, R.A.W., Sarah Binder, and Bert Rockman, eds. 2006. *The Oxford Handbook of Political Institutions.* Oxford: Oxford University Press.

Rimmerman, Craig A., ed. 1996. *Gay Rights, Military Wrongs: Political Perspectives on Lesbians and Gays in the Military.* New York: Garland.

– 2002. *From Identity to Politics: The Lesbian and Gay Movements in the United States.* Philadelphia: Temple University Press.

Rozell, Mark, and Clyde Wilcox. 1997. Conclusion. In *God at the Grassroots, 1996: The Christian Right in the 1996 Elections,* ed. Mark Rozell and Clyde Wilcox, 255–71. Lanham, MD: Rowman and Littlefield.

– 2003. Virginia: Birthplace of the Religious Right. In *The Christian Right in American Politics: Marching to the Millennium,* ed. John C. Green, Mark J. Rozell, and Clyde Wilcox, 41–59. Washington: Georgetown University Press.

Rymph, Catherine. 2005. *Republican Women: Feminism and Conservatism from Suffrage through the Rise of the New Right.* Chapel Hill: University of North Carolina Press.

Saletan, William. 2003. *Bearing Right: How Conservatives Won the Abortion War.* Berkeley: University of California Press.

Sartori, Giovanni. 1976. *Political Parties and Party Systems: A Framework for Analysis.* New York: Cambridge University Press.

Scammon, Richard, and Ben Wattenberg. 1970. *The Real Majority.* New York: Coward-McCann.

Schaller, Michael, and George Rising. 2002. *The Republican Ascendancy: American Politics 1968–2001.* Wheeling, IL: Harlan Davidson.

Schneider, Gregory L. 2003. Conservatives and the Reagan Presidency. In *Reassessing the Reagan Presidency,* ed. Richard S. Conley, 68–94. Lanham, MD: University Press of America.

Scruton, Roger. 1984. *The Meaning of Conservatism,* 2nd ed. London: Macmillan.

Segal, Hugh. 1997. *Beyond Greed: A Traditional Conservative Confronts Neoconservative Excess.* Toronto: Stoddart.

– 2006. *The Long Road Back: The Conservative Journey in Canada, 1993–2006.* Toronto: Harper Collins.

Skillen, James. 2006. Personal interview with author. 31 January. Washington, DC.

Smith, Miriam. 1999. *Lesbian and Gay Rights in Canada: Social Movements and Equality Seeking 1971–95.* Toronto: University of Toronto Press.

Smith, T. Alexander, and Raymond Tatalovich. 2003. *Cultures at War: Moral Conflicts in Western Democracies.* Peterborough, ON: Broadview.

Solinger, Rickie, ed. 1998. *Abortion Wars: A Half-Century of Struggle, 1950–2000.* Berkeley: University of California Press.

Spalding, Mathew. 2006. Personal interview with author. 9 January. Washington, DC.

Stackhouse, Reginald. 2005. Personal interview with author. 10 November. Toronto.

Stanfield, Robert. 1969. Speech to the House of Commons, 25 February. *Commons Debates,* 28th Parliament, Session 1, volume VI, 5919–20. Ottawa: Queen's Printer.

– 1974. Memo to Progressive Conservative Caucus: The Meaning of Conservatism. National Archives of Canada. MG 32 C21.

Steinmo, Sven. 2001. The New Institutionalism. In *The Encyclopedia of Democratic Thought*, ed. Barry Clark and Joe Foweraker, 130–40. London: Routledge.

Stevens, Geoffrey. 1973. *Stanfield*. Toronto: McClelland and Stewart.

Stiller, Brian. 1997. *From the Tower of Babel to Parliament Hill: How to Be a Christian in Canada Today*. Toronto: Harper Collins.

– 2003. *Jesus and Caesar: Christians in the Public Square*. Kitchener, ON: Castle Quay.

– 2005. Personal interview with author. 24 February. Toronto.

Sullivan, Andrew. 2007. *The Conservative Soul: How We Lost it, How to Get It Back*. New York: Harper Collins.

Tatalovich, Raymond. 1997. *The Politics of Abortion in the United States and Canada: A Comparative Study*. Armank, NY: ME Sharpe.

Teller, Paul. 2006. Personal interview with author. 23 February. Washington, DC.

Thelen, Kathleen. 1999. Historical Institutionalism in Comparative Politics. *Annual Review of Political Science*, 2: 369–404.

Tuns, Paul. 2005. Personal interview with author. 31 May. Toronto.

United States Congress. 1994. Republican Contract with America. http://www.house.gov/house/Contract/CONTRACT.html (accessed 17 July 2007).

Urofsky, Melvin. 2000. *Compassionate Conservatism: What It Is, What It Does, and How It Can Transform America*. New York: Free Press.

Urofsky, Melvin I., and Martha Martha, eds. 1996. *The New Christian Right: Political and Social Issues*. New York: Garland.

Vellacott, Maurice. 1998. Speech to the House of Commons, 8 June 8. http://www2.parl.gc.ca/housechamberbusiness/ChamberHome.aspx.

Viguerie, Richard A. 1980. *The New Right: We're Ready to Lead*. Falls Church, VA: The Viguerie Company.

Viguerie, Richard A., and David Franke. 2004. *America's Right Turn: How Conservatives Used New and Alternative Media to Take Power*. Chicago: Bonus Books.

Waddan, Alex. 2002. *Clinton's Legacy? A New Democrat in Governance*. London: Palgrave.

Wagner, Teresa R., ed. 2003. *Back To the Drawing Board: The Future of the Pro-life Movement*. South Bend, IN: St Augustine's Press.

Wald, Kenneth, and Allison Calhoun-Brown. 2007. *Religion and Politics in the United States*, 5th ed. Lanham, MD: Rowman and Littlefield.

Wappel, Tom. 1998. Speech to the House of Commons, 9 October. http://www2.parl.gc.ca/housechamberbusiness/ChamberHome.aspx.

Warner, Tom. 2010. *Losing Control: Canada's Social Conservatives in an Age of Rights*. Toronto: Between the Lines.

Watson, Justin. 1997. *The Christian Coalition: Dreams of Restoration, Demands for Recognition*. New York: St Martin's.

Wattenberg, Martin. 1991. *The Rise of Candidate Centered Politics: Presidential Elections in the 1980s*. Cambridge, MA: Harvard University Press.

Watts, Dianna. 2005. Personal interview with author. 16 June. Ottawa, ON.

Wearing, Joseph. 1981. *The L-Shaped Party: The Liberal Party of Canada, 1958–1980*. Toronto: McGraw-Hill Ryerson.

Whitaker, Reginald. 1979. *The Government Party: Organizing and Financing the Liberal Party of Canada, 1930–58*. Toronto: University of Toronto Press.

Whitaker, Robert W., ed. 1982. *The New Right Papers*. New York: St Martin's.

White, John Kenneth. 1990. *The New Politics of Old Values*, 2nd ed. Hanover: University Press of New England.

White, Theodore H. 1965. *The Making of the President, 1964*. New York: Atheneum.

Wilcox, Clyde. 1992. *God's Warrior's: The Christian Right in Twentieth Century America*. Baltimore: Johns Hopkins University Press.

– 2000. *Onward Christian Soldiers: The Religious Right in American Politics*, 2nd ed. Boulder, CO: Westview.

– 2002. Whither the Christian Right? The Elections and Beyond. In *The Election of the Century and What It Tells Us about the Future of American Politics*, ed. Stephen J. Wayne and Clyde Wilcox, 107–25. Armonk, NY: M.E. Sharpe.

– 2006. Personal interview with author. 12 January. Washington, DC.

Wilcox, Clyde, and Carin Larson, 2006. *Onward Christian Soldiers? The Religious Right in American Politics*, 3rd ed. Boulder, CO: Westview.

Wilcox, Clyde, Linda M. Merolla, and David Beer. 2006. Saving Marriage by Banning Marriage. In *The Values Campaign: The Christian Right in the 2004 Elections*, ed. Clyde Wilcox, John C. Green, and Mark J. Rozell, 56–79. Washington, DC: Georgetown University Press.

Will, George. 2006. Telephone interview with author. 9 March.

Wiseman, Nelson. 2007. *In Search of Canadian Political Culture*. Vancouver: UBC Press.

Wolfensberger, Dan. 2006. Personal interview with author. 10 January. Washington, DC.

Wolfson, Adam. 2006. Personal interview with author. 19 January. Washington, DC.

Wolinetz, Steven. 2002. Beyond the Catch-All Party: Approaches to the Study of Parties and Party Organization in Contemporary Democracies. In *Political*

Parties: Old Concepts and New Challenges, ed. Juan Linz, Jose Ramon Montero, and Richard Gunther, 136–5. Oxford: Oxford University Press.

Woolliams, Eldon. 1969. Speech to the House of Commons, 23 January. *Commons Debates,* 28th Parliament, Session 1, volume V, 4725–35. Ottawa: Queen's Printer.

Woolstencroft, Peter. 2000. Some Battles Won, War Lost: The Campaign of the Progressive Conservative Party. In *The Canadian General Election of 2000,* ed. Jon Pammett and Christopher Dornan, 91–113. Toronto: Dundurn.

Young, Katherine K., and Paul Nathanson. 2004. The Future of an Experiment. In *Divorcing Marriage: Unveiling the Dangers in Canada's New Social Experiment,* ed. Daniel Cere and Douglas Farrow, 41–63. Montreal and Kingston: McGill-Queen's University Press.

Young, Lisa. 2000. *Feminists and Party Politics.* Vancouver: UBC Press.

Index